Rise in Purpose
A Guide to Personal Freedom and Finding Your Purpose

Donese K. Gordon

Copyright © 2023

All Rights Reserved

ISBN: 978-1-961804-07-4

Dedication

This book is dedicated to my son, Grant Antonio Payton. I love you, kid. I thank you for leading me to Christ and helping me to find my purpose. I will never forget you, and I will make sure that your life and legacy will forever live on. You will always live on earth through me until I meet you in heaven.

Acknowledgment

First and foremost, I would like to thank God for turning my pain into purpose. I also want to thank my daughter, Tierra, for sticking by my side despite the obstacles that we faced, and a huge thank you to my team for helping me with the production of this book series. Without you, it would not have been possible.

Contents

Dedication iii

Acknowledgment iv

About the Author vi

Preface viii

Introduction ix

Chapter 1: The Hand I Was Dealt 1

Chapter 2: The Day My Life Changed Forever 13

Chapter 3: The Dream 22

Chapter 4: The Truth 30

Chapter 5: The Letter 38

Chapter 6: The Wilderness 49

Chapter 7: Sanctification 56

Chapter 8: The Shadows of Death 65

Chapter 9: Faith over Fear 72

Chapter 10: Forgiveness 79

Chapter 11: Prayer 87

Chapter 12: Purpose 95

Chapter 13: Addictions 103

Chapter 14: Fruits of the Spirit 110

Chapter 15: Don't Look Back 116

Chapter 16: God's Glory 124

About the Author

Donese Gordon is an Atlanta native who has dedicated her life to serving God and others. She is the mother of two children, a philanthropist, business owner, career counselor, youth mentor, and a warrior for Christ. She enjoys spending time with her family, long walks in nature, cooking plant-based meals, and reading inspirational books.

Preface

My 16-year-old son, Grant, was a victim of senseless gun violence on May 29, 2018. Grant had recently started his first job, and three weeks later, his life was taken from him. I was filled with anger. I begged God and pleaded with God to help me. The pain was too much for me to overcome on my own. Through the tragic death of Grant, he not only healed me but turned my pain into purpose.

Introduction

My unwavering faith is the most fundamental attribute of my personality. Probably, it's the first thing people tend to notice about me. Whenever I find myself engaged in a conversation about religion, I'm met with one of these three responses: admiration, ridicule, or exasperation. However, when I share my beliefs with the world, my only purpose is to inspire hope.

Once, there was a time in my life when I was submerged in a world of utter darkness. No matter where I turned, I was met with despair, betrayal, and rage. Out of desperation, I reached out to my family, friends, colleagues, neighbors, and even strangers. My efforts failed, and I couldn't find the help and guidance I was looking for. It was agonizingly painful to be so vulnerable and ask for help only to get turned away.

It's tragic how every day, countless people give up on their lives after losing hope. I've been there. I know what it's like to not have a single soul by your side to comfort you. When everyone fails you, it's time to look inward to find the source of light from within. It's time to ignite the flame of faith in your heart to get you through the hurdles of life.

In the depths of despair, a single glimmer of light led me through the shadows—the glory of God. There are many people who disregard Jesus Christ in the name of delusions, who mock your beliefs, or who give up on Christianity after multiple attempts to connect with God. There are many who have suffered so much they find it impossible to put their trust in a higher power. Why would God put me through this? Will this suffering ever come to an end? What have I ever done to deserve this hell? When your life feels like it's nothing short of eternal damnation, one tragedy followed by another, then nothing motivates you to seek out God.

Admittingly, I hit rock bottom when I lost my son to gun violence; however, I can hardly recall any joyful memories from my childhood. Since I lost my parents at a young age, I was adopted by my great-grandmother. I was never showered with love like a child craves and needs. Throughout my childhood, I always felt unwanted and unworthy of love. Of course, carrying this damaged self-esteem into adulthood didn't do well for my dating experiences. One toxic relationship followed another until, eventually, I ended up alone.

My past continued to haunt me, but I counted my blessings. Because I had a beautiful daughter and son, I always managed to pull myself together after every rough breakup or financial setback. That is, until I lost one of them.

No affirming words could change my unhealthy behaviors. No counselor could help me navigate that unbearable pain. No support groups made me feel any less lonely. There was a wall that separated me from the rest of the world, so I coped the only way I knew how—by escaping.

It wasn't enough. The pain would seep into my consciousness through my nightmares. The memories haunted me, and I knew eventually, I had to face them. However, when I decided to accept reality head-on, I wasn't alone. When I was ready to seek God, he embraced me with love and led me along the way. At every hurdle, I heard him speak to me. Every time I was betrayed, he helped me get back on my feet. At every discouraging comment, he gave me strength to brace it. At every suicidal thought, he reminded me of my purpose.

With God's guidance, I learned to face the terrifying darkness and rise from the dead. God's words spoke to me when everything else failed, so let this book be a source of hope and guidance when you feel like giving up. Remember, you're not alone because God is only a prayer away.

Chapter 1
The Hand I Was Dealt

"God decided in advance to adopt us into his own family by bringing us to himself through Jesus Christ. This is what he wanted to do, and it gave him great delight."

(Ephesians 1:5)

For as long as I can remember, I have worn a mask to protect myself and my feelings from this cruel world. Not everyone knows how to fight back when they're trampled upon and treated poorly by others. When we feel disrespected, unvalued, or invalidated, we can't help but lash out. Most children throw a tantrum to get heard, while adults try to resolve the conflict by yelling over one another. However, some of us are silenced before we get a chance to demand. We accept our misfortune, put up a smile, and retreat into a protective shell that only provides us temporary solace.

One day, I gathered some courage and decided to remove this mask of self-preservation, only to find the self-destruction that was hidden underneath it. In our day-to-day lives, we rarely ever analyze our actions to realize all the ways we sabotage ourselves. It can be impossible to be mindful of your actions, especially when you've spent all your life suppressing your pain. When you grow up feeling worthless, you accept the bare minimum from people, let promising opportunities pass, and only escape the sense of failure that follows by further engaging in self-sabotaging behaviors.

Eventually, these self-sabotaging habits catch up to us, and we're forced to face reality with all its brutality and imperfections. There's only so long a person can dwell on everything they've lost. After a while, the comfort zone that once lulled us into a false sense of security starts to feel suffocating. Nothing feels more terrifying than the dark void of stagnation. You watch everyone move forward in life while you're stuck in the same desolate place. You try and adjust, but it just seems like you can never keep up with those people. Realizing that they are way ahead of you leaves you feeling out of place and hopeless.

Once I acknowledged this truth, there was no way I could turn a blind eye, and it started tormenting me. I knew I had to pull myself together, even if it took every bit of strength in me. I made a vow to God that if he helped me to find peace within, I would share my truth to help others.

Even before suffering the greatest loss of my life, my childhood wasn't particularly pleasant. I was adopted at the age of four years old and never knew my biological parents. When you don't receive proper parental love, the feelings of low self-worth haunt you for the rest of your life. No amount of love, reassuring words, or grand gestures ever seem enough, despite your strong yearning

RISE IN PURPOSE

for just that. You always crave love from others to feel complete, but your desperation only leaves you feeling emptier, like a void that can never be filled.

For an adopted child, it's only natural to struggle with this mental anguish. Given how tragically I lost my mother, it not only impacted how I perceived the world but also how I was treated by my family. My mother was killed when I was four years old, and my younger brother was two.

When a misfortune strikes a family, it leaves more victims than one. Nearly everyone is terrified of premature death. When a person dies young, they are robbed of their future and often a chance to say farewell to their loved ones. Their unexpected and early demise traps their grieving loved ones in the limbo of agony. No matter how hard they try to escape, a part of their soul dies alongside the victim. After experiencing the same tragedy as my grandmother, I can completely understand her attitude toward me following my mother's death.

Throughout my childhood, I always felt unwanted because my grandmother, who lived in New York, decided to adopt my little brother and not me because I looked just like my mother. Once I grew up, I learned to understand her anguish and empathized with her loss. However, as a child, I failed to understand those complex emotions. Although I was too young to comprehend death, I could feel the loss of my mother. Without her by my side, I felt even more sensitive and vulnerable about how I was treated. *Why*

doesn't my grandmother want me? What's wrong with me?
Such thoughts plagued my entire childhood, but I had no one to hear me out.

My grandmother could not deal with the pain of losing her only daughter and looking at me every day, so she sent me to live in Atlanta with my great-grandmother. I felt abandoned and rejected by her. I couldn't help but blame myself for not being accepted. When you are adopted, you miss the attachment and feelings of love, and you always feel alone, no matter how much love you have around you. Through several heartbreaks, I learned this the hard way.

When you grow up feeling unwanted, you internalize the belief that something's wrong with you. Because I did the same, I started bending over backward to make up for those "flaws"—to fix whatever was wrong with me. I did everything to prove my worth, just for acceptance. I believed if I compromised on all my desires and pleased everyone around me, I could buy their love. I was at my wits' end, tired of life and trying to prove myself to people for love. The people I was trying to prove myself to definitely didn't deserve to have me in their life.

Despite my struggles, I thought I had it all figured out— this thing called life. Because I navigated this world wearing a mask, I thought I could get through my entire life the same way. Fake it till you make it. Right? I believed so. I thought I could make my relationships work if I just put in enough effort. I believed I could ignore the void in my chest, suppress years of trauma, and move on with life. I truly believed I could live my life in denial until my son was a victim of senseless gun violence. Losing Grant turned my world upside down. I could neither face the pain nor ignore it. When I tried to escape it, the relief was only temporary, and the anguish returned far more amplified than before. This merciless reality was an eye-opening experience that pulled me out of my self-destructive life.

If only I knew God like I know him now, things would have been different in my life. I wouldn't have turned a blind eye to the realities of life. I would have never let ANYONE make me feel less than a person. I would have faced the hardships instead of escaping them. I would have been kinder and more forgiving toward myself and others. I would have turned to God for help, walked away from toxic relationships, and given my kids a better life. I would never have let meaningless grudges destroy my mental peace. We all have moments where we could have done things better; however, you learn from your mistakes, and if God leads you to something, he will bring you through it.

All my life, I have yearned for unconditional love. I sought it from my family and searched for it in relationships, only to find that no one could love me the way I needed. I always felt unloved and unwanted, but I discovered through the Bible that God loved me so much that He adopted me into His spiritual family as a chosen child of God through his son, Jesus Christ. After years of mindless search, I found this love that I should've looked for in the first place. Loving God and building a relationship with Him brought me the strength to continue striving when I felt despair. It brought me solace when I felt restless and guided me when I felt lost. It gave me the courage to walk away from people who mistreated and disrespected me. Most of all, it taught me how to forgive and move on.

Today, I no longer harbor resentment in my heart for people who have wronged me. I can find it in myself to overlook their shortcomings, set my sights on the positive aspects, and appreciate all they have done for me. I love my grandmother and miss her dearly. I wish I had the opportunity to tell her that I don't blame her for not raising me and that I now know it was all a part of God's plan for my life. Forgiving people filled my heart with the love I had searched for almost all my life. Just this radical understanding of her sufferings and acceptance of my own feelings was enough to bring me peace.

During my childhood, her rejection greatly affected my feelings of negative self-worth. Although her poor treatment contributed to many sufferings in my life, I no longer blame her. However, after everything I've endured, I realize how foolish it is to wallow over what you couldn't have. Now I hold myself accountable for my circumstances instead of using my traumatic past as an excuse. Like most people, I never let the environment of my upbringing, being adopted, or feeling unwanted

RISE IN PURPOSE

define me. I always kept going, no matter what life threw at me.

"Fear not, for you will not be put to shame; And do not feel humiliated, for you will not be disgraced; But you will forget the shame of your youth, And the reproach of your widowhood you will remember no more."

(Isaiah 54:4)

I grew up feeling so invisible that I never reached out for help. Even when things were extremely tough, I tried to find a solution on my own. Despite never speaking up or seeking help, I always felt like I was taking too much space. Mostly, this self-reliance helps build character; however, it can also often lead to a fear of speaking and a lack of communication. When you feel worthless, every minor mistake feels like a huge crisis. I was always beating myself up over meaningless things, so how could I bring myself to reveal something life-changing? This is probably why I chose to hide from my family when I experienced the first major crisis of my life.

I became pregnant with my daughter when I was seventeen years of age, and I was simultaneously filled with shame and happiness. A part of me was happy that I was about to have my own family, and the other part was ashamed because of what others thought of me. At the age of seventeen, this fear is quite natural. When I had no support from anyone, how could I truly rejoice? The uncertainty of my future filled my heart with dread. I was

7

scared of the tremendous responsibility that had fallen on my young shoulders, but the fear of being shunned by society was far more overwhelming. So I hid my pregnancy until I could not hide it anymore—until finally, I had started to show, which led to my adopted mother asking me about it, so I reluctantly told her.

A few days later, a family member came into my room while I was sitting on my bed. My worst fears were coming true because she looked at me with disdain. In a reproving voice, she said, "You are so stupid! You should have told somebody, and my momma could have taken you to have an abortion." What a way to comfort an already terrified young girl! I could already hear the mocking remarks, the jeering laughter, and their judgmental comments. They couldn't understand the anguish I was going through.

My heart sank at her words, and I cried myself to sleep that night. From that day forward, I became even more ashamed, and uncertainty was added to the storm of my emotions. I knew I would have to take care of my daughter by myself. I knew I couldn't expect any support from my family. I realized no one would accept me, but one thing I was certain of—I would take care of my child by any means necessary, even if it cost me my own happiness. I vowed to nurture my child with so much love that she would never have to go through the same desperation I did.

I was in excruciating pain after I gave birth to my daughter and was told by a nurse that she had stopped

RISE IN PURPOSE

breathing and was immediately rushed to the neonatal intensive care unit. When they finally allowed me to see her, there were tubes everywhere. The mere sight of her lying there in that condition scared me. The doctor informed me that she had a very slim chance of survival without complications. I was terrified out of my wits, but I was alone. Although I had no family to support me, I managed to pull myself together. I was discharged from the hospital while my daughter was still admitted. I decided to go to church the following Sunday.

During the entire church service, I prayed and begged God to please allow my daughter to live without complications. While I was praying, all the uncertainties and doubts escaped my mind. Everything I had feared regarding parenting seemed insignificant to me. I didn't care if I had to do it all alone; I had been doing that almost my entire life, and I just wanted my daughter to live. Tears trailed down my face as I told Him that if He allowed her to live, I would work hard to take care of her and be the best mother I could possibly be. My desperation came through, and my prayers were answered.

The next Friday, she was released from the hospital with a clean bill of health. At that moment, my heart was filled with gratitude, and I realized this entire ordeal was a lesson from God. It was a way to give me clarity and strength, so I wouldn't live with regrets later on. Getting to hold my baby girl was exhilarating, and I was overcome with joy. She was so tiny and beautiful. I promised myself that I would always be there for her and protect her from all harm.

Shortly after giving birth to my daughter, I moved into my own apartment with her father and secured a job. I grew up so fast that I mentally went from seventeen years of age to thirty. In that time of uncertainty, God paved a path for me. Despite all my fears, it all worked out for me because I kept faith in God. I was married to my daughter's father at twenty-two and became pregnant with Grant at twenty-four.

I never forgot the words that family member said to me that day, and the feeling of shame that came over me made me stronger. I would say to myself, *One day, I will be successful and give my kids the best life I possibly can.* Since that day, I have drawn strength from every critical remark. Whenever someone demotivated me, I felt challenged to prove them wrong—to work my way up.

My family was complete, but I wanted to provide financial stability to my children. I wanted a career where I could make a lot of money and have the flexibility of providing for my children, so one day, while I was at work, God led me to research the staffing industry.

I came home from work that day and told my kid's father that I was quitting my job to start my own agency. Of course, he thought I was nuts. He thought I was just being impulsive and wouldn't follow through with my plans. I

RISE IN PURPOSE

was met with the same response I had received from my family for years. I was made to question my decision, but I have always been a person who jumps headfirst into whatever I feel passionate about and is never afraid to take risks. I didn't know that much about staffing, but I knew that I could do anything I put my mind to, so I quit my job.

Shortly after, I went to work for a staffing agency, and the manager was impressed with my passion for the job and loved my energy and enthusiasm, so she hired me, knowing I had no prior experience in staffing. Before they could even train me properly, I was already bringing in new clients and putting people to work. Although I was far from reaping the rewards of my hard work, I did not lose hope. Soon after working there, I met another diligent person who would later be my business partner. She shared my optimism and dedication, and we decided to start our own agency.

At home, I was on the verge of losing everything. Things kept piling one on top of another. Our cars were repossessed, the house was in foreclosure, the electricity was cut off, and I remember my friend telling me that my kids' father told her I was stupid for quitting my job. Once again, I was met with discouragement instead of support. Because of my husband's disapproval, I felt alone in my struggles. I was crushed, but I was determined to prove him wrong, so my business partner and I worked day and night until we finally started making money.

My dedication pulled us out of the financial crisis we were in, but I lost all respect for him for not believing in me. I had silently endured far too many years wearing a mask to please everyone around me. Once the mask slipped, I couldn't put it back on. I had to regain my self-respect, and in order to do that, I had to sever that bond. Unfortunately, our marriage didn't last.

The fact that people thought I was stupid for taking a risk pushed me to pursue a dream that I now know was a part of my purpose. It was one thing to get ridiculed by society, but to hear the same from my own husband was heartbreaking. There was no risk bigger than having a daughter at seventeen, but I risked it without knowing how I was going to take care of her. I got married, not knowing if it was going to last, and started my own company with no money and no knowledge of how to run a business.

If the things I just listed made me stupid, then I don't ever want to be smart. I have made a lot of mistakes in the past, but I never allowed my mistakes to stop me from taking risks. This courage and passion pulled me through the most challenging times. There have been times when I was afraid I would lose everything, but I didn't allow it to stop me from taking the risk. All of those lessons, losses, heartaches, and risks were God's way of preparing me for my destiny.

I always knew, deep down inside, that God would provide for me and that He would be there for me, no matter what.

Chapter 2
The Day My Life Changed Forever

"You intended to harm me, but God intended it for good to accomplish what is now being done, the saving of many lives."

(Genesis 50:20)

Each year, millions of teenagers in the U.S. lose their lives to violence. Today, in America, gun violence has surpassed car accidents as the most prevalent cause of death. The world forgets, and people move on, but these tragedies continue to haunt the families of the victims for the rest of their lives. It's impossible to ever move on from such a loss. Every single day is a victory in itself when you're being pulled by death. No matter how many years pass by, how many tears we shed, and how many consolations we get, it is never enough.

On May 29th, 2018, my son, Grant, became one of those statistics. He was a victim of senseless gun violence. My eyes still well up with tears as I pen down this horrible truth.

How do you find solace when you lose your child to a brutal murder? How do you pull yourself together when you lose your purpose in life? How do you survive when everyone abandons you in your hour of need? How do you accept the injustice of losing the person you brought into this world—your beautiful child you raised with so much love, devotion, and care? Imagine if you had to ask yourself these questions, would you have survived? Would you have made it to the other side, from darkness to light?

The moment you give birth, you start to have dreams for your children. These dreams inspire you to work harder to make this world a better and safer place for them. So, you put in all your efforts to nurture them, to provide them with emotional and financial stability, and to raise them into good and respectable citizens. You constantly worry if they will grow into healthy adults. You wonder if they will take after you or their father, if they will succeed academically, and what they would like to become when they grow up. All your plans revolve around your children's wishes and desires. When all these hopes and dreams are shattered before they can take shape, there's no way of recovering from the heartbreak.

I will never forget that night I received that knock on my door. I still remember walking up to the door, blissfully unaware of the horrors that awaited me. I had no idea how my life was going to change forever. When the news broke, my entire body, including my mind, went numb. A terrifying chill was spreading throughout my chest. I was traumatized and overcome with anger. *How dare they say my son wasn't alive anymore...*I couldn't process what I was being told.

RISE IN PURPOSE

"Gunshot... Grant... Dead..." I believed it was a jumble of senseless words pieced together to torture me. Perhaps a sick joke.

I tried to piece the words together, but no matter how hard I tried, I couldn't believe my ears. They were trying to communicate with me—to comfort me. *What are these empty consolations? What do they mean by that?* It just wasn't possible. *Grant, my son! He's going to come home soon. He doesn't stay out past curfew.* Helpless sobs were escaping from my mouth despite my disbelief. *He's a good kid!* I expected him to walk through the door, to surprise me, and to tell me it was all a horrible joke.

Once I realized Grant was not coming home, I wanted to disappear. I wanted the ground to swallow me up. I couldn't possibly live without my son. It was completely out of the question. How could I continue living knowing he wasn't sleeping in the room next door? It all felt so wrong, so devastating, and so impossible. Nothing made any sense. I didn't know how I was going to survive the most devastating pain a person could ever experience in life.

My disbelief turned to despair. I became nothing but an empty shell of a person. I went about my tasks mechanically while trying to hold onto any semblance of sanity. Soon, I couldn't stand that stagnation and my despair was replaced with rage. *How could God do this to Grant? What did I do to deserve this hell on Earth?* I can honestly say that I know personally what hell feels like. I don't ever want to go there again.

The death of a child is bad enough by itself, but to have somebody murder them for nothing is a whole different type of pain. When you lose someone you love, it feels unjust; you blame fate for taking them away. Some days, you want to die to reunite with them. However, when I found out my child was murdered, my heart was filled with vengeance. Whoever was responsible for Grant's death, I wanted them to suffer. I wanted them to experience the same pain I felt. I remained restless throughout the nights, plotting a way to get justice for Grant. Every day, I fought an inner battle with the monster raging in my chest.

With every passing second, a million regrets plagued my mind. I imagined how he must have felt. I imagined him feeling desperate, lonely, and helpless. I imagined him bleeding to death, lying helpless in a pool of blood. *Was he crying out for help? Or did he lose consciousness? Was it painful? Did he find peace in the end?* I couldn't help obsessing over his pain, tormenting myself in the process.

When my son had gone out, I couldn't have imagined never seeing his sweet smile again. How could I have known? The safety of children is the most prevalent concern in every mother's mind, yet the thought of this nightmare never crosses their mind. It's too terrifying to entertain for even a second. I didn't have the chance to say goodbye to him or tell him I loved him for the last time. I

RISE IN PURPOSE

was devastated. I cried myself to sleep every night, obsessing over everything I would have done differently to save him. For hours, I ruminated ways I could have stopped him from leaving the house that night. Could I have my son by my side if I had done things differently?

After Grant's funeral, I was hospitalized for a week and then sent to a mental institution for two weeks for further evaluation. No matter how hard I tried to pull myself together, the pain was too much to bear. I couldn't break out of my state of denial. Initially, I lost my faith after losing my son. I had no source of hope to support me. Neither could I find a friend in man or God anymore. Every time I tried to pray, I only felt bitterness, rage, and hatred for the fate I had to endure. *If there was a God out there looking out for us, then why was my child stolen away from me? Why did Grant have to die?* Although my faith was questioned, I pushed myself. I doubted everything in life, but deep in my heart, I knew I had found my true calling.

Shortly after my release from the hospital, I received a call asking me to pick up Grant's death certificate from the funeral home. I remember reading it and seeing that his cause of death was a "gunshot wound to the left thigh." That was the first moment I had fully acknowledged this reality. Although my eyes welled with tears, I vowed to get to the root of his murder. I don't remember much after that other than turning into a private detective overnight. I didn't dwell on my grief because only one thing mattered— bringing Grant's killer to justice.

The house where Grant was hurt was less than two minutes from the police station, and it took them over thirty minutes to get there. Grant bled to death, and his life could have been saved if he had received help sooner. When this information was revealed to me, I could not contain myself. Just finding this out filled my heart with rage. I did not want to see sense. I couldn't help but blame anyone and everyone involved in his case. I just wanted all of them to suffer. My kid didn't deserve this. If not for the incompetence of the police force, my kid would have been alive and by my side.

I was so distraught; I spent every second finding clues. I could not do anything but try to find out how to get justice. I listened to all the 911 calls related to the incident multiple times, viewed Grant's crime scene photos, and contacted multiple attorneys. Every detail in every photograph traumatized me further. This investigation consumed my nightmares, and I could only see the horror repeating itself every night in my dreams.

All the attorneys I contacted thought Grant's case was not worth their time because of the sovereign immunity law in place in Georgia. Officers and emergency personnel are not held responsible for showing up at a crime scene within a certain time frame. Basically, they get there when they can. I just couldn't accept this truth. These people had to be held accountable.

RISE IN PURPOSE

Once I got back on my feet, I found my faith. Getting back on my feet was far from simple, but my desire for vengeance gave me strength. I started praying, hoping to find a solution. There wasn't much else I could do besides helping the officers fill in the gaps. Without a culprit, I could either look for someone to pin the blame on or take everything in stride and plan justice for my son with a rational mind. Previously, I had done nothing but the former, but with every desperate prayer, I found strength within myself to fight for my son.

Finally, after contacting numerous attorneys, God led me to one who offered to help me and take Grant on as a client. I felt a little relief once I found an attorney. However, I was so traumatized by the information that I immediately sank into a major depression. I was forced to abandon my pursuit—the only purpose I had managed to find. My entire world turned upside down once I uncovered the truth.

More than anything, I struggled to get by in life without listening to his voice. Sometimes, I would hear him calling me out, and I would rush into his room to find it deserted and his bed neatly made. Those days, I dragged my feet into his room, sat on his bed, and burst into tears. The longing to see his face, hear his voice, and hug his frame was so unbearable it suffocated me.

My entire life was built around his needs, happiness, and dreams. My daily routine started and ended with taking care of my children. Every second of the day, I was reminded of him. His favorite food, songs, shirt, everything sent me down a haunting spiral of memories. I missed Grant so much and could not imagine my life without him. It was like a constant throbbing ache in my chest. Whenever I tried to distract myself, my thoughts drifted back to him.

I had never experienced that type of pain before in my entire life, and I would not wish it on my worst enemy. After everything I've overcome, I wouldn't even wish it on Grant's murderers. Although I've overcome many challenges, I could never bring myself to part with him. I refused to bury my child. Some may think I am nuts, but when you love your kids the way I love mine, you will never accept some things, and death is one of them. Given how I lost my son, it is impossible to move past it. It might seem creepy, even unorthodox, to many, but it seemed like the natural course of action to me.

I fought hard and sacrificed much to keep Grant's legacy alive. When I look at all that my purpose has helped me endure, I don't regret any of it. I had to drag my feet at every step, fighting negative opinions, judgments, and my own inner demons. I didn't care what I had to go through. I was determined that Grant's life mattered, and he would not be just another figure in the statistics. It was the only way I could find some peace.

Before Grant's death, I would crumble under stress and breakdown like any other human being. However, this tragedy changed me for the rest of my life. When you've

RISE IN PURPOSE

already experienced the worst life can possibly offer, nothing deters you. There's no challenge you can't face because every struggle pales in comparison. It's a long journey, where you face victories and defeats every day, yet every victory is unimaginably significant. Only the victims of such traumatic events can understand the pain and the endurance. When the limits of your resilience are stretched, you start to perceive the world through a different lens. You evaluate every hardship, taking appropriate measures to overcome it, until you become immovable, like a mountain.

When I failed to find answers, God showed me how I could find comfort despite my doubts and fears. When there was no hope, I learned to pave my path with a sense of purpose and ambition. I reminded myself of everything I had promised Grant. I want to keep my word to him. I want to change this cruel world so no mother has to endure the pain I had to go through. After everything I have endured, I want to fulfill my purpose—to become a beacon of hope for those who are struggling to even hold on to life.

Chapter 3
The Dream

"In a dream, in a vision of the night, when deep sleep falls on men, while they slumber on their beds."

(Job 33:15)

Anyone who has lost a loved one can understand the terrifying grip of despair. The feeling consumes you every waking moment. The instant you open your eyes in the morning, the deep aching pain in your chest keeps you from getting out of bed, so you lie there for hours. Time passes by, but nothing moves you. You're stuck but desperate to escape with no escape in sight. Possibly, everyone has experienced this anguish, but not everyone has overcome it. Many people turn to drugs and alcohol to numb the pain and spend the rest of their lives unable to face what they've lost. It takes courage to accept reality and break out of that endless despair.

Nothing compares to the feelings of helplessness following the death of your child. Every second passes in search of a distraction, anything to get your mind off the emptiness that continues to haunt you. You feel desperate to latch on to an activity or a person to escape the painful memories. However, no matter how hard you try, your loss remains at the back of your mind. Like a zombie, you engage in activities mechanically while your mind remains elsewhere in a dark, haunted place. The feeling torments you. It eats at you until you learn to fight back.

After losing Grant, I turned into a ghost with no strings holding me to this life and reality. I yearned to be with him and to hear the sound of his voice. Everything I did was a reminder of my child's untimely death. When I went out to eat, I thought about his favorite food. When I listened to songs, his favorite melodies haunted me. When I went shopping, I found myself stumbling into the boys' section. Every place and person was a painful reminder of him, tormenting me with the horrible truth I couldn't escape.

Nothing was left that could make this world worth living in with the exception of my daughter. I tried to pull myself together for her. I tried to remind myself that she had lost her brother just as I had lost my son. It can be incredibly challenging to support your family members when your own scars haven't healed. I knew my self-destructive behaviors, indifference toward her pain, and hopelessness were difficult to deal with. I knew by hurting myself, I was hurting my daughter in the process. However, my growing desperation kept fueling my despair. I have always lived for my children; however, without Grant, I simply lost every motivation to live for her and myself.

In times of hopelessness, reassuring words from friends and family start to sound completely hollow. Even though you want them to reach out, you want someone to rescue you from that abysmal void, but a part of you knows they can't. Whenever you're offered reassuring words, the despair reels you into the void deeper than before. Every kind word is a reminder of how it will never be okay. Their attempts to help only expands the disconnect, dividing you from the rest of the world.

"I'm sorry for your loss." *Thanks, I guess. I don't know what else to say.*

"Everything will be alright." *You don't possibly mean that, do you? No, it won't be okay. I don't think so.*

"Keep faith in God." *Faith in God? How? Seriously, after what I've been put through? Don't make me laugh.*

Every time I was met with these pointless condolences, I felt flames of rage and resentment burning in my chest. Of course, I never expressed my thoughts. I put up a smile, a perfect mask for the rest of the world, and suppressed my voice. I thought it would work and I would be able to connect with others, but it didn't. How could it ever possibly be okay? How could someone else even begin to understand the depth of my suffering? How could I keep faith in God when Grant had been taken away from me? How could I pull myself together when I had no desire to live? I felt like an ocean separated me from everyone else. When their voices failed to reach me, the disconnect only added to my bitterness.

RISE IN PURPOSE

Gradually, we start losing our faith in God, the faith that had sustained us through life. We only go to church on Sundays and seek God out of desperation. Oftentimes, we're so selfish we only pray to him when life throws difficulties in our path. In times of despair, we want to pray, but no words come out of our mouths.

When I turned to prayer, I would pray for my daughter; however, when I would try to pray for myself and Grant, my mind came up blank. I found no purpose in praying. No prayer could bring him back to life, and nothing could ease my pain, so what was the point of seeking God? *I can't pray for my son's health, safety, success, and happiness anymore.* Every time I raised my hands in prayer, I would realize how little I had to be thankful for and how desperately I had to search for a reason to smile. The prayers only reminded me of every source of happiness I was stripped of.

When I reached the depths of my despair, I settled in that darkness. I stopped fighting or trying to escape. For days, I would lie in bed without taking a shower or having a proper meal. I had completely abandoned myself. I grew comfortable in my state of isolation and stagnation until it became too much for me. If I had a choice, I would've stayed there, but life doesn't allow it. Human beings have an inner drive to grow, to move forward, to socialize, and to make progress in life. One can only wallow in misery for so long. No one can spend their entire life shunning people, rejecting life, comfort, and happiness.

Eventually, we all begin to yearn for salvation because human beings can't help but struggle for survival. It's our nature to seek challenges to fight the feeling of discontentment.

Once we are ready to reach out, God helps us pull ourselves together and get back on our feet. No matter how long we spend in despair, His love shines through the darkness. All we have to do is ask for forgiveness and pour out all our feelings before God. We just need to turn to Him, and since communication is a two-way street, we should initiate it first. The answer might not come fast, but it will in due time. Believe me. He might speak to us in dreams to give us signs and wonders.

I was in so much pain, mentally and physically, and could see my chances of survival growing thinner. Although my daughter was worried about me, I couldn't care less about life. I just craved the sweet relief of death to run away from my problems. I had started abusing alcohol to escape reality. I would get drunk so I could fall asleep and not think about it. My self-destructive behavior continued until, one night, Grant came to me in a dream. Just seeing my son's face again, I was overcome with emotions. Everything was so vivid—his sweet face, his frame, his voice—I couldn't tell it from reality. Even in my dream, I knew Christ would save me.

I remember that night like it was yesterday. Something had triggered me, and all the suppressed emotions had come up again. For hours, I sobbed into my pillow, tossing and turning, hoping to find some relief. Of course, crying didn't help, and that much sought-after relief remained out of my reach. I remember going into the kitchen, grabbing a bottle of alcohol, and downing half a bottle of Jack Daniels. I remember how I collapsed on the couch in my living room and drifted off to unconsciousness. I remember the feeling of warmth replacing the ever-persistent cold.

The darkness was replaced by a bright blue sky and lush green plains. The intense, burning pain in my chest turned into a dull throb, and soon, it was replaced by a state of peace. My eyes drifted from the vast plains on my left to the sight of a boy standing ahead. How could I not recognize him? Grant was standing by a river, and I was so close to him that I could touch him. I remember being filled with excitement and running toward him.

"Are you okay?" I asked him, locking him in a hug. I couldn't believe I could touch him!

He responded, "Yes, I am okay. My Father has been feeding me fish and okra." As he said this, he pointed at the river. I felt confused, but Grant had a serene smile playing on his face.

I turned around in the dream and saw a shadow of a person who, in the dream, I thought was Grant's biological father. Almost instantly, I grew protective of my son. *Why is he standing there like that?* So, I asked him loudly, "Who do you think you are, Daniel Boone or something?"

I said it so loud that I woke up from the dream with the name still sitting on the tip of my tongue. *Daniel Boone,* I whispered to myself, sitting up in my bed. For the first time in so long, the weight of the sorrows over my shoulders didn't hold me down.

I kept thinking about it all day. I hadn't smiled that much in a very long time. All day, I kept replaying the dream in my mind and how peaceful Grant looked. I kept thinking about the sound of his voice and holding him in my arms. In fact, it might have been the first time since his death I felt genuinely happy. It was enough to bring me back to life.

Even a few days after the dream, I couldn't get that name out of my head. I kept saying it, trying to interpret the meaning. The questions possessed my mind day and night. *Did I know someone who went by that name? Did he ever harm Grant? Was this a sign from God, or was I reading too much into things?* So, I decided to take some time to analyze my dream. Previously, I had only considered dreams as random images playing in our subconscious mind. Whenever I heard someone talking about dream interpretation, I laughed and thought to myself, *What a joke!* However, I couldn't help but read more into my experience, so I researched *Daniel Boone,* and to my surprise, I found out he died on Grant's birthday. It was all I needed to confirm my theory—the universe was giving me a sign!

RISE IN PURPOSE

Daniel Boone loved the Lord and devoted his life to worshipping Him. In 1816, he wrote, "The religion I have is to love and fear God, believe in Jesus Christ, do all good to my neighbor and myself that I can, do as little harm as I can help, and trust on God's mercy for the rest."

Water symbolizes God's value of life and is essential to all living things. I didn't go too deep in trying to understand the fish and okra part because I knew the dream was from God, assuring me that Grant's spirit was with Him and that he was perfectly fine.

I did not know it at the time, but the dream was confirmation and a special revelation to me of God starting His purpose of redemption in my life. I cannot express how that dream changed me. I could pull myself together because I knew Grant was in a better place. One day, I would be reunited with him. A glimmer of hope burnt bright within me, but my life took a drastic turn for the worse shortly after the dream. Or so I thought.

Chapter 4
The Truth

"All things have been committed to me by my Father. No one knows the son except the Father, and no one knows the Father except the son and those to whom the son chooses to reveal him."

(Matthew 11:27)

"Jesus said to him, I am the way, and the truth, and the life. No one comes to the Father except through me."

(John 14:6)

People who think they are wise and reject God are blinded to the truth. Instead, the ones dismissed by the world and called foolish are revealed to the truth. Jesus knows the Father who had given the information about "all things" to him.

The relationship between God and Jesus is profound. God has placed all his knowledge within Jesus, but only those who want to listen to the word of God will be able to listen to the truth; others will stay astray.

RISE IN PURPOSE

"Now we can see that you know all things and that you do not even need to have anyone ask you questions. This makes us believe that you came from God."

(John 16:30)

When all seems lost in this fast-paced world, the grind doesn't stop for anyone, and if we want to achieve something in life, we have to keep hustling, but amidst all this, we have lost touch with our faith. What is the truth of life? No one knows.

Many people find their peace in Christ. The hope for salvation feels like a healing balm to a wounded soul. When you feel disconnected from the world, knowing that God is looking out for you can keep you going forward. But how do we revive our lost faith? His disconnect is deeper than we have ever imagined. Logic and reasoning have got the best of us, so faith seems impossible to restore. We tend to sway from things if there's no logical explanation for it.

But how does one explain faith? It's like following a dark path, knowing in your heart that there will be light at the end of it. That's faith, and there is no logic behind it.

Most people mock Christians who actually follow Christ. "Your beliefs are not grounded in reality. There's no scientific evidence supporting your claims," they say. They do not understand that Christianity is not the same as religion. It teaches you how to connect with God, and it is God's way of saving humanity. It is more about creating a personal relationship with God and his creations around the world and the universe. Most people do not understand the difference and question us and our faith.

However, while they continue to reject our Christian values, they struggle all their lives to find their purpose. They yearn to find some peace, trying to fight off the restlessness that accompanies the need to solve every mystery. No one puts faith in Christ without some level of contemplation, but we learn to accept what we have no way of knowing and what we can't have. Our *"blind"* faith protects us from the turmoil that comes with the Faustian sacrifice because questioning everything only leads to eventual misery.

The truth is, our faith is guided by a way of life that has worked for people all over the world for centuries. It is cemented by signs and wonders when we seek out Christ for help. It is built on the foundation of the feelings of tranquility, hope, and love which result from our faith. Mostly, the people who find peace within themselves, who live a life full of contentment, are firm believers of Christ.

Despite the glaring benefits of following Christ, Christians get a bad reputation. Mostly, it's the people who condense Christianity into a bunch of inflexible rules. As a kid, when I did something wrong, I was told God was going to get me. I was taught at church and home to run from

RISE IN PURPOSE

God, instead of running to Him, because of fear that He would punish me.

Some leaders of Christianity don't have a real relationship with God, so their teachings are ego-driven. They tend to instill fear in their members, but in doing so, they are drawing people away from God. Yes, fear is the best tool the enemy will use to gain control over your life.

How can you expect a child to head in the direction of precisely what they fear? Moreover, this fear was instilled in me by those religious sermons that were supposed to strengthen my faith. I knew that Jesus died on the cross for my sins, but because of what I was taught, I thought I was being punished for things that I did wrong. It's true that while love motivates us to grow, fear motivates us to avoid punishment only.

The Bible tells us to fear God, but it isn't the kind of fear that tells us to be scared of Him. The fear of God that the Bible talks about means obeying Him, treasuring Him, and following Him. You fear God in the sense that you let Him rule your life.

"Now when all the people saw the thunder and the flashes of lightning and the sound of the trumpet and the mountain smoking, the people were afraid and trembled, and they stood far off and said to Moses, "You speak to us, and we will listen; but do not let God speak to us, lest we die."

"Moses said to the people, "Do not fear, for God has come to test you, that the fear of him may be before you, that you may not sin."

"The people stood far off, while Moses drew near to the thick darkness where God was."

(Exodus 20:18–21)

Every time I got hurt, I lost myself in a spiral of thoughts, recalling everything I did wrong. To some extent, this belief helps discipline children and builds character. However, when a person's faith is built on the foundation of fear, their good values remain restricted to a sense of approval. They fail to find any peace of mind or salvation in religion. I didn't know Jesus and didn't have knowledge of His grace and mercy, so I never thought to turn to Him for help.

I worked for a well-known communications company in Atlanta, Georgia, for six years. During my wilderness season, something happened to me that I will never forget. It was something that nearly shattered my faith.

While talking to one of my co-workers about God, I mentioned Jesus to her, and she looked at me like I was crazy. Her reaction was beyond my understanding; why was she looking at me like that? The next words that came out of her mouth crushed me. She said, "What are you talking about? God doesn't have a son."

RISE IN PURPOSE

It was the way she said those words, in a matter-of-fact tone, contradicting everything I had ever learned. When people criticize someone's faith, they fail to realize how our beliefs are woven into the fabric of our being. They fail to realize how many nights we have spent crying all alone with nothing but our faith keeping us alive or how many times our belief has saved our lives in times of despair.

From that day forward, I started to doubt God and withdrew further from him. I stopped praying like I used to, and I lost all hope. *Why is this so difficult? Why am I laughed at when I'm on the right path? What's the eternal truth?* My wavering faith only added to the anguish I was already going through. It didn't seem plausible that God would turn me into a Jesus Joker when I was in the right.

When Grant passed, I remember thinking I had a better chance of believing in Santa Claus than God. If God loved me, why didn't He stop my kid from being murdered for nothing? Why was He putting me through this? I needed Jesus more than anything, but how could I turn to someone for help who I didn't believe existed?

Questions are good. Curiosity is even greater. If you don't question, how will you learn? So, when all these questions, filled with pain and hatred, emerged in my mind, I didn't know I was on the right path. I was clueless to know that sooner or later, I would get my answers. I was also unaware of the fact that questioning your beliefs isn't all that bad.

Consider faith as a fruit plant. When the fruit starts to grow on its branches, all kinds of insects and birds try to peck at it. While all this tugging and pecking may leave the fruit bruised and scarred, that is how the plant grows and starts producing more fruits. All this struggle is only to make your faith stronger.

I cried out to God one day. I begged for Him to help me, and He sent Jesus Christ to save my life. Jesus not only saved my life, but He changed it. He gave me purpose and overcame Satan's attempt to destroy me. He gently led me out of the darkness that had consumed my life.

The only way to the Father is through the Son, and if you don't believe in the Son, you will not have salvation.

If you have started asking hard questions about your faith and go to God for answers, know that you will eventually be visited by Jesus Christ, just like I was. Faith isn't static; it has to take different shapes and change with us. As we grow up and realize the truth behind our lives and the purpose of it all, the face of faith changes. It would either grow strong or fade away, but if you have even a molecule of belief, you will find your way back.

I will never forget the day I felt like someone had finally pulled back the curtain, revealing what I already knew to be true but had forgotten. Once again, I was enlightened, and all my doubts cleared away. I am grateful for the experience.

RISE IN PURPOSE

Jesus died for all of us so we can have eternal life in God's kingdom and peace on earth. You shall know the truth, and the truth shall set you free. Jesus Christ is the way to your salvation and freedom. Trust me. I am a living witness of His grace, mercy, power, and love.

Chapter 5
The Letter

"And Hezekiah received the letter of the hand of the messengers, and read it: and Hezekiah went up into the house of the LORD, and spread it before the LORD."

(2 Kings 19:14)

There is no timeline for the process of healing. I know it is widely believed, but people start to grow weary of your mourning. Those exasperated heavy sighs never go past your notice. Their frustration makes it seem like they're suffering in your place, doesn't it? One by one, you notice how these people leave your side, how they tire of your existence, and sometimes, go as far as stabbing you in the back. This world has no patience for anyone, especially not for a grieving mother. I realized it the hard way, so I had to pull myself together.

Some traumatic events are so earth-shattering that the wounds they leave never get healed. One day, you wake up to a bright sun with elevated spirits, thinking you've recovered. You feel sure-footed, eager to move ahead with the world, but even a minor setback takes you right back to where you started—back on your knees. No matter how many times you talk about your grief, no matter how or where you channel that energy, the painful feeling in your

RISE IN PURPOSE

chest lingers for the rest of your life. Unpacking traumatic events and processing those tormenting emotions can only do so much to help with your pain.

A strong will, dedication, and optimism are not enough to pull you through. You need something more—something unwavering, like faith in God. No one stays by your side when you're at your lowest, but you can always count on God to guide you through the darkness.

Therapy doesn't work for everyone. Letting out those years of pent-up emotions might work for a while until something triggers those haunting memories. Many other factors can hinder your progress in therapy, sometimes, your self-sabotaging behavior. Before you know it, you can't save yourself from falling; you relapse. You spiral out of control and head down that path of self-destruction and self-loathing. Feelings of hopelessness start to consume you once again. Once again, you start to numb the pain, escape reality, and become the most toxic version of yourself. Once you stifle the voice of your conscience, your actions only leave destruction in their wake. The feelings of remorse follow only a little too late.

Most of us prefer to drink our sorrows away. If it's not a bottle of alcohol, then it's the abuse of other mind-altering substances. One way or the other, we develop life-long addictions to escape the horrors of reality. Once we go down this path, we only keep spiraling out of control until there's no way to save ourselves. One way or the other, it only ends up in tragedy.

I started drinking heavily during my first marriage, and I didn't seem to be doing any better on my second failed marriage either. Once again, I broke down under stress and started drinking and smoking every day. Although I hit rock bottom after losing Grant, my unhealthy coping patterns had already developed in his life. My low self-esteem and traumatic childhood only worsened my condition. Grant could see that I was slowly killing myself and my future. It's incredibly heartbreaking for a child to see their mother like that. Of course, I wasn't proud of my behavior, but these patterns had been cemented for so long that I couldn't help myself. Even though I had given up on myself, he always believed in me, no matter how many mistakes I made during his short time on earth.

Grant was so worried about me that, at the age of fourteen, he wrote a letter to me and taped it to the liquor bottle. It's a huge burden to put on the fragile shoulders of an adolescent boy, but he always loved me, nonetheless. It was a tiny attempt to help me—a simple gesture of love that, although I appreciated tremendously at the time, I couldn't bring myself to honor it. When I discovered the letter, I immediately took a picture of it, threw the letter in the trash, and continued to go down this dark path. After he passed away, my initial response to his thoughtful gesture broke my heart. He must've felt like his efforts were in vain; however, it made me all the more determined to honor his words in death.

RISE IN PURPOSE

Some people never want to take accountability for their actions. They would rather push people away than change their habits because even the thought of facing reality is too challenging. It's far too terrifying to accept your mistakes, your past, and the injustice that has followed you all your life. Although I didn't want to be reckless with my actions, I felt too weak to keep putting in the effort. Every time I tried to get back on my feet, something would knock me over, and I would end up giving up on the future. I would give up all the work I had put in and just quit. Only when the time had slipped by did I allow myself to acknowledge the value of those little things I lost.

Two years after Grant passed, I was in a deep depression over his senseless death. I was doing exactly what my son had cautioned me against, and my condition was a disgrace to his wishes. I drank every day, smoked cigars, took prescription medications, and lived on social media. My life revolved around suppressing my sorrows, feeding my resentment, and engaging in harmful behavior. I couldn't help but give up on the concept of growth and self-improvement. When I just couldn't bring myself to take any interest in life, how could I work on myself?

No matter what I did or tried, I could find no solace in anything. Nothing worked for me, even if I tried to change my ways—just for Grant's sake. I kept trying to find engagement in other activities, seek support, and think positively, but it just wasn't working out for me. I lost interest in everything I had once found enjoyable because Grant's death was always at the back of my mind. His memories didn't leave me alone for a second. No matter what the topic of the conversation was, my mind would always return to only one subject—my son's death. Returning to a stable life had become so unattainable it seemed like a pipe dream. My mind was gone, my health was deteriorating, and I had no peace whatsoever.

When I had given up all hope, I started seeing signs from God that became my salvation. From dreams to distorted memories, I kept seeing signs guiding me, so I kept praying. One day, I was weeping alone, cursing myself for throwing away that letter, when I recalled taking that picture. I had captured it in my drunken state, so the picture had completely slipped my mind. However, as the memory flashed before my eyes, I found myself going through my gallery with a newfound sense of purpose. Ever since Grant's death, it was the first time I had felt a glimmer of hope. Thankfully, God led me back to the letter and revealed that it was my blueprint for my salvation and freedom.

In Grant's letter, God revealed to me these key points:

People use the stuff they drink to burn down houses by getting a bottle with the drink in it, putting a towel in it, lighting it, and throwing it to burn down stuff.

"Jesus is the light of the world, turn to him for help."

RISE IN PURPOSE

"When Jesus spoke again to the people, he said, "I am the light of the world. Whoever follows me will never walk in darkness, but will have the light of life."

(John 8:12)

Stop buying all the liquor, wine, beer, and cigarettes.

"Ask Jesus to heal me and to free me from all addictions."

"Come to me, all you who are weary and burdened, and I will give you rest. Take my yoke upon you and learn from me, for I am gentle and humble in heart, and you will find rest for your souls. For my yoke is easy and my burden is light."

(Matthew 11:28-30)

There are other ways to make yourself feel good. Even though these things temporarily make us feel better, they are far more harmful in the long run. Taking care of ourselves makes us feel better, and it obviously has no bad consequences. Get your nails done. Start grooming yourself, and you'll start to feel better about yourself.

"Ask Jesus to teach me how to love and care for myself."

"Do you not know that your bodies are temples of the Holy Spirit, who is in you, whom you have received from God? You are not your own; you were bought at a price. Therefore, honor God with your bodies."

(1 Corinthians 6:19-20)

You need to focus on your staffing business. You need to get back to work. Engaging in activities might feel impossible right now, but when we are faced with responsibilities, we are left with no choice but to pull ourselves together. The longer you stay wallowing in your distress, the more challenging it will be to get back on your feet.

"Ask Jesus to bless my business and lead me into my purpose."

"Just as the Son of Man did not come to be served, but to serve, and to give his life as a ransom for many."

(Matthew 20:28)

RISE IN PURPOSE

LETTER FROM GRANT – May 25, 2016

READ ALL OF IT!

DONESE K. GORDON

Don't ever pick up a glass of wine again. I really think you are addicted to drinking liquor, wine, and beer. I think you overdrink, and you fill the whole cup full of liquor, beer, and wine, which is bad. You can't blame anyone but yourself. You say we make you mad, but that don't mean you have to smoke five cigarettes and drink 1/3 of liquor, beer, or wine. I don't think you understand how cigarettes affect you each minute. Cigarettes make you feel good, but then, in 5 minutes, you start feeling depressed. That's why you keep getting another one because you want to feel good, but there are other ways to make yourself feel good. The liquor, beer, and wine are the reason you are so violent. People use the stuff you drink to burn down houses by getting a bottle with the drink in it, putting a towel in it, lighting it, and throwing it to burn down stuff. Your heart rate is decreasing every day; it may not feel like it, but I promise you it is. You complain that you don't have any money, but if you stop buying all the liquor, wine, beer, and cigarettes, you will probably have money to get your nails done. But you probably don't listen to me, but don't say I didn't warn you. You need to focus on your staffing business. But if you ignore this letter, you are going to have to press a button just so you can talk.

This letter was a call of awakening for me. Once, I had felt annoyed with those words and disregarded them. Honestly, I felt defensive. *Who does this kid think he is? Who is he to judge me or decide what's good or bad for me? He doesn't understand what he's talking about.* My overdefensive thoughts kept me from seeing things

46

sensibly. We rarely ever listen to our children, much less pay any attention to their reprimanding words. In fact, we are so egotistical that our pride gets hurt. Although I felt irritated, I was genuinely touched by his concern.

Once, it had broken my heart to see the roles switched. However, children have wisdom that most people fail to recognize. Though they can't always call us out, they can sense when we go astray. They can tell when something has gone so wrong it starts to affect our daily lives. Their minds may not have developed enough to communicate effectively, but they feel just as strongly as us. They feel uncertain, fearful, and concerned about us. We should never invalidate their feelings or make light of them. Instead of feeling ashamed, we should form a strong bond with our children, learn to communicate with them, and teach them to voice their thoughts. Just because they lack experience, there's nothing wrong with valuing their advice.

Eventually, the feeling of guilt overpowered my despair. Every time I would pick up a bottle of alcohol, Grant's words would flow through my mind. Every time I engaged in self-harming behavior, his concerned face would flash before my eyes. Nothing could possibly be more wrong than consuming alcohol to keep the ever-lingering thought of my son out of my head. I realized his mother should be honoring his memories more than anyone else instead of trying to suppress them. I was supposed to keep his legacy alive instead of destroying myself along with it.

Nothing could be more unfair to him than escaping those memories because facing them was too painful.

So, I drew strength from these words, pulled myself together, and managed to overcome my addictions one by one. Every step was uncertain, but I kept moving. Every time I felt like giving up, I reminded myself I wasn't alone because God was supporting me all the way. Whenever I faced a setback, instead of reaching for a mind-altering substance, I reached for that letter. Grant couldn't leave me with a farewell letter, but he left me with more than that— God and hope for a better future.

Chapter 6
The Wilderness

"Remember how the LORD your God led you through the wilderness for these forty years, humbling you and testing you to prove your character, and to find out whether or not you would obey his commands."

(Deuteronomy 8:2)

All of us go through a wilderness season in life. They are the experiences of oppression, grief, attacks, and rejection. Some of these leave us shocked and embarrassed, draining us emotionally. Though these times would make us miserable, a blessing is hidden in them. It is a blessing from God, who wants to test our faith.

The troubling times spent in the wilderness have a purpose—to correct and teach us.

"When Pharaoh let the people go, God did not lead them on the road through the Philistine country, though that was shorter. For God said, 'If they face war, they might change their minds and return to Egypt.' So, God led the people around by the desert road toward the Red Sea. The Israelites went out of Egypt ready for battle."

(Exodus 13:17-18)

God knows of our strengths and of our weaknesses. He created us, so he knows of our capabilities, which is why he leads us through tough paths, guiding us every step of the way. He is aware of our abilities to cross certain paths and shows us the correct way—the one we can walk on easily.

The journey toward salvation and enlightenment is never easy. You meet many hurdles along the way. Some of these are troubles of our own making—the twisting web of negative thoughts that keep us looped into those harmful coping mechanisms. However, other times, life puts us through such excruciating experiences we can't help but go astray. Every door seems to get closed, and the only path ahead left to take is a dark and lonely one. It can be impossible to hold on to faith when you're lost.

I consider myself blessed because every time I went down a wrong path, a glimmer of light always guided me toward righteousness. It took some time and a tremendous level of resilience, but I managed to make it. I kept hearing the voice of God tell me to trust the process and keep going. There is a process that Jesus has, and if you follow him and keep his commands, you will be set free. You have to die first and be born again, following his instructions closely. You have to go through a rite of passage. You might feel like you would suffocate with the intensity of the pain. You might feel like the pain is so unbearable that death would be a better alternative. However, if you trust the process and don't give up, you will experience victory in every area of your life.

RISE IN PURPOSE

The process is rigorous, and though it is jaw-breaking, it is the path of glory. Only the ones who stand tall in the face of challenges will receive the ultimate gift from God. Then and only then will you understand the purpose of life and of your existence. Then, you will learn the true meaning of life. It will be a life of light dictated by God. With faith and immense love in your heart, you will be able to live a life bearing the gift of God's love at every step.

The process is surely hard, but it is worth it. Once you get there, you realize all you were missing in life. Many people spend their entire lives simply yearning for that peace of mind, but they fail to achieve it. They don't trust in the healing process and give up before they can reach the other side. If you follow Jesus from beginning to end, you will make it to the other side. On the other side is your freedom, your salvation, and access to God's kingdom on earth.

My wilderness season started when I turned fourteen years of age and ended when I was forty-six. Like every teenager, I felt apprehensive about all the changes taking place in the world around me. This fear was amplified when my adoptive father was diagnosed with cancer. When I was fourteen years old, he passed away from prostate cancer. I watched him slowly deteriorate—slowly slipping into what I then saw as a dreadful void. I watched him grow weaker, and one day, I returned home from school, and his bed was empty. Just like that, he was gone forever.

Before he left, he asked my neighbor if she could adopt me because he was dying and wanted to make sure that I was taken care of, and she did. It wasn't enough—being taken care of wasn't enough. A gaping hole in my heart was left by the people who had once occupied that spot. From that day forward, I have never trusted anyone but myself. I never felt comfortable around anyone, so I never opened up. If I ever tried, I lived in a state of constant fear. Thinking that they would be snatched away from me—it drove me insane.

I am probably one of the few people who would ever admit this, but I don't regret my past. Yes, I've made mistakes that I later lamented on. I have hurt people, and people have hurt me. However, I believe there is a purpose for everything. I made it to where I am today after every good and bad thing I have experienced, and although I would never change it, I would never want to live through it again.

I'm not proud of every awful thing I've done. Nor would I ever try to justify them, but my actions have always been a reflection of my experiences. I drank a fifth of liquor every three days, smoked like a chimney, took anti-depressants and stimulants, ate horribly, and bathing was not in the picture. *Who can possibly tolerate this behavior? Who would love me when I'm such a mess?* Instead of working on my way of living, I indulged in those negative thoughts. My fiancé left me, people I thought were my friends and family turned on me, and I was left all alone.

RISE IN PURPOSE

I was at the point of no return until I finally broke down and begged God to help me. When I was down and I called for help, only God heard me. He heard me regardless of my awful activities because he sensed a spark of hope and faith in my heart. I wanted to be found, to be saved, and to be held by the light of God. So, I begged and begged. I didn't do it for anyone other than myself and my children.

Toward the end of my wilderness season, God put me into isolation, and it was the loneliest, lowest place I had ever been in my entire life. But it made me stronger. That's when I realized I didn't need anything other than God's love for survival. The more I meditated on God's word, the more I discovered the truth of who I was in Jesus Christ and the price He paid for my sins. I learned to love myself in His sacrifice because I finally knew how much He loved me.

I suddenly found myself at the mercy of God, my creator, my heavenly Father, the one I had placed on the back burner. All these years, I ran from God when I should have been running to him. I was so humbled. When God was all merciful, what had I been fearing all this time? What drove me away from God all those years? I learned to count my blessings instead of letting resentment build in my chest. I begged God for forgiveness and for him to help me change for the better. I was sick and tired of being sick and tired.

Wisdom and understanding of God's word do not come naturally. If you only have your eyes trained on evil, pain, and suffering in life, you will not be able to see the light beyond. You have to ask him for it in prayer, and he will surely give it to you. The day after my fiancé left me suddenly, I cried out to God in prayer for Him to help me because I was devastated and did not understand how he could do such a thing. He failed to honor his commitment, and I failed to pull myself together until a light bulb went off in my head.

I got out of my bed and wiped my tears. *I've survived worse than this,* I reminded myself. *No matter what I go through, God will always be looking after me.* When we seek guidance from God, we don't need to look far. You start to see the reflection of His love in a beautiful sunset, a child's smile, a comforting friend, and most importantly, in the verses of the Bible. This is what happens when you recognize faith within yourself. If you remain blind toward it, you will never be able to step out of the wilderness and will be forever wandering within the darkness that it has to offer.

To escape my agonizing thoughts, I immediately opened the Bible app on my phone. The following verse was staring me right in the face:

"I will send you the helper from the father. The helper is the spirit of truth who comes from the father. When he comes he will tell you about me. And you will tell people about me too, because you have been with me from the beginning."

(John 15: 26-27)

RISE IN PURPOSE

To come out of the wilderness, you must look for signs. The signs could be hidden in anything and everything. God can choose any aspect of your life to teach you a lesson, to guide you out of darkness and into the light. You just have to take a deep breath, hold onto your faith, and use it as a torch to step out of what has been holding you back.

God used my failed engagement to lead me to John, then John led me to Jesus, and then Jesus set me free. As He tested me and pruned me, I had no other choice but to follow Him and His directions for my life. I was humbled enough to know that God was in control, and I desperately needed His grace and mercy. I am very thankful that I was obedient to His voice as He freed me, humbled me, healed my broken heart, and led me to my purpose. I experienced pure intimacy with God and grew closer to Him.

Chapter 7
Sanctification

"The God of peace will himself sanctify me completely."

(1 Thessalonians 5:23)

The Lord who began this process of sanctification the moment that my heart was made alive to him *"will bring it to completion at the day of Jesus Christ."*

(Philippians 1:6)

"And that is what some of you were. But you were washed, you were sanctified, you were justified in the name of the Lord Jesus Christ and by the Spirit of our God."

(1 Corinthians 6:11)

Sanctification is the transformation where Christ and the Holy Spirit work together to help you become Christlike—to become holy. Of course, we can't ascend to that level of purity and holiness. It's impossible to reach that height of righteousness. However, if we let Jesus guide us, if we follow his teaching, we can reach the destination of this holy journey.

As children, we innately imitate the values taught by Jesus Christ. In our innocence, we always remain truthful and loving. In our naivete, we share love and kindness with

RISE IN PURPOSE

our neighbors. Despite life's hurdles, we find a glimmer of hope. However, as we grow older, the demands of life pull a curtain before our eyes. We harden our hearts to shield ourselves from the sufferings of the world. Our lifelong resentments lead us astray from our path. They deviate from our true calling and blind us to what truly matters in life—our salvation.

Sanctification is personal and different for every believer. We're all walking a different path in life, so our challenges can lead us to dissimilar actualization. For some, it means giving up a life of luxury and devoting themselves to God's services. Others might reach a level of enlightenment where they no longer care about meaningless sorrows. They accept every challenge life throws their way and keep faith in the best outcome. Instead of cursing their fate, they practice patience and start to see a purpose behind God's ways. It liberates them from the fear of disappointments and heartbreaks. While some just accomplish peace of mind by learning to forgive themselves and others. They find it within their hearts to rise above the conflict.

God uses the difficult things in our lives to strip us of ourselves and have us dependent solely on him. Sanctified souls have endured, learned, and accepted this truth. Their minds no longer remain burdened with uncertainties and fears. Although the path before them might be tough, they remain steady in their steps because they know their steps are ordered by God.

Only when we have been stripped of everything we hold dear do we begin to achieve that level of transformation. Only then do we realize how utterly meaningless our concerns had been. We come to a life-altering realization that none of our worries matter in the grand scheme of things. Everything had been planned out for us by God; we just have to hold on to our faith and keep moving forward.

God stripped me down to nothing. Jokingly, but seriously, I didn't even have a roach. I didn't have anything to hold on to. I didn't have anyone to support me as I continued losing everything I considered valuable in life. God removed everyone from my life, one by one. Family, friends, neighbors, colleagues—every single person abandoned me eventually. The person who I thought was my best friend betrayed me, and God allowed it to happen because He wanted me to end the friendship. He wanted to burst my bubble and pull me out of my false sense of security. My friend revealed their true colors because God wanted the truth revealed to me.

When I was trying to mend my broken heart, God accelerated my healing journey by enlightening me. Around the time I was trying to cope with my friend's betrayal, I felt an instinctual pull. Although I didn't understand it, I gave in to it. During this whole ordeal, God led me to a pizza restaurant that sold various plant-based pizzas. In my ignorance, I thought I was there to speak to the owner and order dinner. Of course, why else would I

RISE IN PURPOSE

have mindlessly stumbled into a pizza restaurant? But God had other plans for me.

When I arrived, I walked up to the counter and asked for the owner. I remember offering the cashier a smile. "Hello, can I speak to the owner of this place?"

The cashier didn't return my smile. Instead, she rudely told me that the owners did not have time to speak to customers. "Sorry, can't help you with that. We'll take your order if you want something." She couldn't care less about my concerns, and I was about to let her have it when I heard a voice telling me to stay silent. I can't explain how, but I knew it was God's will. I knew what was required of me. It was a bizarre sensation, but I did as I was told. I bit my tongue, patiently stood in line, and waited for my turn to order food.

The lady next to me struck up a conversation, and I began to share Grant's story with her. He's all that I could talk about, and I was so lonely I couldn't help but pour my heart out. In that moment of weakness, I decided to be vulnerable before a mere stranger, and I wasn't disappointed. The woman was sympathetic and tried to comfort me to the best of her abilities. However, the bizarre turn of events didn't end there. They had only started.

To my surprise, the cashier overheard our conversation, and she blurted out, "You are the young lady!" I just stared ahead, confused. Her attitude had completely changed from before, and she went on to explain, "A woman came into our store two days ago with two bottles of oil. She gave me one and told me that God was sending another young lady for the other bottle in the next two days. I will know exactly who to give it to." When the cashier explained, she looked just as nonplussed as I did. The explanation did nothing to alleviate my confusion, but I knew at once it was another sign from God.

Still confused, I looked at her strangely, but I decided to give in. The cashier didn't seem to have an ulterior motive, and she didn't have a cause to lie to me about something so strange. Reluctantly, I took the bottles of oil and ordered my food. What did I have to lose? Nothing; I was already stripped of everything dear to my heart.

When I arrived home, I went into my purse to retrieve my cell phone. Although the encounter was strange, I had already put it at the back of my mind. Those days, I wasn't fazed by much, but the moment my eyes fell on the oil, I found myself getting goosebumps. At that moment, I heard a voice, and I knew God was speaking to me again. The voice said, "Now anoint your head with that oil. I am anointing you for business, ministry, prophetic teaching, and anything else I instruct you to do for my kingdom. I chose you; you didn't choose me, so you don't have a choice."

"You prepare a table before me in the presence of my enemies; you anoint my head with oil; my cup overflows."

(Psalms 23:5)

RISE IN PURPOSE

Everything I was experiencing was bizarre, to say the least. Many would think I had finally lost my grip on reality and my sanity. Was I bewildered by my experience? Obviously. Did I question my own sanity? Yes, of course, but did I hesitate? No, not at all! I didn't think I had a choice in the first place because some foreign force was stringing me along, gently guiding me to the path of my destiny.

If there is any confusion on free will, let me clear it up for you now: when you are chosen, you don't have a choice. You feel compelled to move, driven by the higher power. All your senses and reasoning fail you. God will bring you to your knees and put you in a situation where you have no other choice but to follow His commands, stay obedient to His words, and allow His will to be done in your life. Nothing will work for you until you surrender completely to Him. He will keep blocking all your paths until you give in—until you decide to walk the path meant for you.

My journey toward sanctification had begun. During the sanctification process, He is pruning and removing things from your life that do not belong. The heartbreaks and betrayals challenged me repeatedly. I was filled with loneliness, depression, fear, and doubt. It seemed like there was no one in this world I could trust. I felt isolated, with only my haunting memories accompanying me through life. I mourned over everyone who had abandoned me, but I surrendered to God as I was meant to.

61

DONESE K. GORDON

During this time, I had no other choice but to draw closer to Jesus, and I discovered that Jesus was all I needed. My isolation didn't matter anymore. No one else mattered, and I no longer evaluated my worth according to how people treated me. I was ready to walk my own path because I was no longer alone. I was being led by Jesus. When you are alone in life, you learn that God is enough, and you don't equate this season with being unlovable, unworthy, unattractive, or not good enough. God doesn't abandon you just because you've hit rock bottom. Instead, you feel His unconditional love more strongly when you're at your lowest.

God wants you alone so that He can fill the voids in your life, heal you from the traumatic experiences of your past, and prepare you for the amazing future He has in store for you. When nothing or no one is enabling or deluding you, you can begin your healing journey without any hurdles. Once you set foot on this journey, the loneliness stops eating at you. You start to face the horror you had previously escaped for years.

When I was younger, I would laugh when I heard older people say they were saved, sanctified, and filled with the Holy Ghost, and now I can't believe I am saying this, but I am, too. I've experienced this transformation firsthand. I've felt my lifelong wounds healing with the power of faith.

When you dedicate your life to Christ, you relinquish everything back to Him: your children, finances, companies, health, mind, heart, and soul. This radical

RISE IN PURPOSE

acceptance replaces all your anguish, doubts, and resentment with peace of mind. You don't need to fight inner battles constantly when you let go and give up control. You don't spend your hours contemplating the 'what ifs.' Because you trust God, a sense of calm replaces all the feelings of unease. Jesus taught me that I had zero control over my life. I don't own anything, and everything I have belongs to God.

When our prayers go unanswered, the first thing that crosses our mind is: "He's not listening. God doesn't exist." It's in that hour of need when our faith is put to the test. Instead of becoming discouraged, we should take it as a sign and pray more. I prayed to God to bless me with additional financial resources, but He did not bless me with them right away. It was right around the time when I was struggling financially the most. I had gone through so much; I couldn't believe I had to suffer through more hardships. My thoughts echoed a single question: *When will it all end?*

Although it often filled my heart with despair, I always reminded myself to hold on to hope again. Jesus showed me how to sow good seeds so I could reap an abundant harvest. I was led to donate a portion of the financial resources I had on hand to various charities monthly, to volunteer at a local food bank, give care packets to homeless individuals, and donate everything I owned before Grant's death to my local Goodwill.

After his death, my faith was put to the test like never before. Grant bought me a pair of shoes for Mother's Day before he passed, and God told me to donate them. I couldn't believe what was being asked of me. The gift was so close to my heart that I wasn't ready to part with it. What could I possibly have gained by giving away a gift from my deceased son? When the thought occurred to me, I hesitated, but the Holy Spirit spoke to me, "Release them. Grant will buy you shoes every year for the rest of your life."

Without thinking twice, I trusted the voice. I gave up what little I had been left with, but my gain was far greater than what I could've asked for. I dropped the shoes off at the Goodwill, and every Mother's Day after that, God blessed me with a new pair of shoes from Grant. You will no longer fear scarcity once you realize that God can and will bless you with everything you need.

Chapter 8
The Shadows of Death

"Even though I walk through the valley of the shadows of death I will fear no evil, for You are with me."

(Psalms 23:4)

"And the God of all grace, who called you to his eternal glory in Christ, after you have suffered a little while, will himself restore you and make you strong, firm and steadfast."

(1 Peter 5:10)

It's a universal belief that you only live and die once. We're told to live uninhibited, experience more, and shun fear because we only live once, but some of us have experienced such unimaginable horrors in life that we might as well have lived twice. The impact of such phases sometimes remains with us, making home deep in our souls. Some of us are lucky enough to die and still continue to live. As I write this statement, I can't help but laugh out loud.

Those who have chosen death over a lifetime again know that many sufferings in life are akin to a slow, painful death. To live is to die because your spirit never dies. When you are called by God to evolve to fulfill the purpose of your life and advance in his Kingdom, your spirit goes through the shadows of death. They are the moments of life that challenge you, push you into the darkest corners, and laugh at you as you try to crawl back to life. And as you struggle to do so, you die a million deaths. It isn't just you who dies; it's your motivation, your courage, and your rigor—everything within you takes a plunge into the abyss of death, and yet you find yourself breathing.

Gradually, everything you had once held dear starts to become pointless. Your personality, preferences, and priorities begin to change. Your old self dies, and only your spirit perseveres. "Jesus Christ died on the cross for you." This statement, which you had taken for granted for so long, takes on a new meaning. His sacrifice signifies your own rebirth so that you can have eternal life.

Transitioning from old to new is one of the scariest, most painful, and loneliest things you will ever have to endure. Nobody likes change, especially when they have become used to the mundane nature of their life. The truth is change never comes easily, but it is worth it if you trust the process. It is also true that the process is what kills us the most. It is like driving on a narrow lane that is swirling up a mountaintop—the twists and turns will definitely make you uncomfortable. They will have you dig your nails into the steering wheel, but it will all be worth it once you get to the top.

The key is not to look back and don't give up, no matter how hard it gets. Although we complain about our struggles, we always thrive in difficulty. No one can be satisfied if they remain stagnant because evolution is our need.

When we go astray, wallowing in our miseries and blaming fate is the easiest route to take. Escaping responsibility sounds like the best option. However, the path to wisdom can only be found when we put in our utmost effort. Like most people, I prayed the Lord's prayer for years and never understood it for a long time.

"Even though I walk through the valley of the shadows of death, I will fear no evil, for You are with me."

(Psalms 23:4)

People relate this verse to death; however, it is an encouragement for the living to keep going as the shepherd (Jesus Christ) leads them through the darkest, most difficult season of their lives. It sends a message of hope rather than despair. There I was, in the dark valley of the shadows of death, all alone by myself. What was my life other than an abyss of hopelessness? It was darkness worse than death.

For years, I called out for help in vain. I tried to claw out of that void, only to fall back deeper than before. My painful struggles only poisoned my heart further until I realized I was exactly where God wanted me to be. It's when we are cornered by difficulties our true selves spring out—the ones that God wants to see. He doesn't want our made-up personalities or the pretentious words of thankfulness; He wants us to tell Him of our pain. He wants to hear our cries, and just when we start pleading, telling Him of our miseries, He catches us. Just like that, He wanted me by myself so I could hear His voice, heal, discover my purpose, and become the woman He created me to be.

For as long as I can remember, I have always suffered from low esteem. My loneliness aggravated my feelings of low self-worth. Right before Grant passed, I was involved in a serious fight with this guy I was dating at the time. Grant and I were sitting at the table, and he looked me dead in the eyes. He said, "Ma, you are too beautiful to allow anyone to mistreat you. I don't care who it is." Coming from my son, those words left a deep impression on me. Although it took me a long time to change my ways, I learned my worth when I found my true purpose and started living it.

When I was in eighth grade, this kid called me "Donese, the nappy-headed beast" every day. Those words followed me into most of my adult life. As I walked through my shadows of death, God spoke to me, "We are about to *unleash the beast.* Do you remember when that kid picked on you when you were younger and called you a nappy-headed beast? Well, we are about to show you just how pretty you are—just how powerful you have always been. I am about to unleash the beast within you."

Although I buried it deep down inside my soul, in my subconscious, I always thought I was not attractive. I always saw myself as undesirable and undeserving of love.

RISE IN PURPOSE

Those taunting jeers haunted me for so long that I saw an unattractive person in the mirror. Because of my low self-esteem, I always got into abusive relationships, but I never realized it at the time.

After everything I have overcome, I hold my head up high. Now that I know who I am in Christ, I would never allow anyone to mistreat me or abuse me. The road to redemption is powerful. If you can endure the trauma, you can endure the path Jesus leads you on for healing. Consider it like a test, something you have to go through in order to enter the heavens. Once you realize the importance of traumas, the reason behind difficult times and miseries, you will find God. You will not only find him but understand his intentions for his creation.

God moved me into a quiet one-bedroom apartment on the north side of Atlanta. A few days after I was settled in, I heard the voice of Jesus encouraging me to walk. I didn't question the voice as a calm feeling descended over me. I just put my coat and shoes on and headed outside. Before I realized where my feet were carrying me, I was led to walk on a nearby nature trail by a river.

As I continued my stroll, I heard the voice again, this time speaking to me directly, "The LORD is my shepherd; I shall not want. He makes pastures; he leads me beside the still waters. He restores my soul; he leads me in the paths of righteousness for His name's sake." (Psalms 23:1-3) I need you to walk until I tell you otherwise.

DONESE K. GORDON

Once again, I did as I was told. I began to walk twelve miles a day, and the more I walked, the more I heard the voice of God. With every step, the voice became louder and clearer. Jesus spoke to me and encouraged me every single day through the Holy Spirit. I was healed through nature, without the help of doctors, therapists, or psychiatrists. Nobody but God brought me out of the depths of darkness. This can only be achieved when you have faith in your heart that God will save you no matter how hard life gets.

Most people step away from God when difficult times arrive. They pray to the lord, and when he doesn't answer immediately, they abandon him completely. In reality, God is testing our patience in such trying times. He wants us to believe in him and hold onto him so that he may guide us once the time is right.

Day after day, my spirits were lifted, and I started feeling encouraged. I stopped drinking, smoking, or taking prescription medication. I avoided social media and refrained from watching the news. Not only did I overcome my addictions, but I also started living a healthy lifestyle. I started a plant-based diet, fasted, prayed, meditated, recited affirmations, journaled, and practiced gratitude. Before I knew it, I was healing and following the path God had planned for my life.

I still don't know which was worse—losing Grant, my wilderness season, or my road to redemption—but I do know that God was with me through it all. No matter what

RISE IN PURPOSE

your situation is, Jesus can and will heal you. If Jesus hadn't shown me those signs, if He hadn't led me to light, I wouldn't have survived. I would've succumbed to that darkness. I would've let those unhealthy coping mechanisms destroy me or take my life.

God helped me, and He will help anyone who seeks salvation. All you have to do is believe. Ask Him with petition through prayer, and He will come to your rescue. The hardest thing in the world is to remain thankful when you have lost so much, especially the death of your child, which can wreck you for life. How can you be grateful for anything when the very thing you want the most cannot be given back to you? I remember God telling me, "I can't give you Grant back, but I will bless you double for your trouble, and with the desires of your heart, you just have to trust me."

Loss is inevitable and something that can't be replaced sometimes. But God is great. Just like He replaced my loss with gratitude, He will fill your hollowness with something much better. You just have to be patient and wait for His call.

From that day forward, I started to thank Him for everything in my life. I learned that you have to thank Him when you are up and thank Him when you are down. So, I challenge you to go to God in prayer today. Seek Him out, and ask Him to unleash the beast within you.

71

Chapter 9
Faith over Fear

"Have I not commanded you? Be strong and courageous. Do not be afraid; do not be discouraged, for the LORD your God will be with you wherever you go."

(Joshua 1:9)

"Fear not, for I am with you; be not dismayed, for I am your God; I will strengthen you, I will help you, I will uphold you with my righteous right hand."

(Isaiah 41:10)

"I have given you authority to trample on snakes and scorpions and to overcome all the power of the enemy; nothing will harm you."

(Luke 10:19)

When I talk about God's grace, people often think I was raised with this unshakeable faith. They think I have been following Christ all my life. They think I had a strict upbringing, maybe. Why else would someone consciously choose to adhere to something without any evidence? Sometimes, in their ignorance, people simply assume I must

RISE IN PURPOSE

not have endured enough to still hold on to something so abstract so firmly. Of course, they couldn't be more mistaken.

Neither was I raised with this gift, nor have I ever taken it for granted, and I certainly have seen enough suffering to question the existence of God. I acquired this faith by battling my thoughts and struggling to attain it for years. I don't just practice my faith out of habit. Building a relationship with God requires resilience. It takes courage to blindly put all your trust in God, to let Him guide you through life, and to accept all the challenges He puts in your path. Most of all, it requires consistent efforts, even when your faith wavers and you don't feel like going forward.

Despite all the struggles, there are many who never doubt God's love. When the darkness of despair clutches at their hearts, their resolve only strengthens their belief. Nothing brings them more solace than their love for God. As a matter of fact, their belief in God is so strong they don't need any support from anyone else. I applaud everyone who has had an unwavering faith, but for me, that was not the case. Time and again, I did not just give in to my despair but also raged against everything God would put in my path. I refused to accept my bitter reality and either escaped or fought against His will for my life.

God kept telling me, "I am going to help you. You just need a mustard seed of faith." I turned my ears away from His guiding voice and turned a blind eye to all the signs.

Sometimes, cryptic messages are not enough to rekindle the spark of hope. When we have been disappointed a little too many times, an optimistic message or a symbolic dream doesn't guide us toward salvation. A person who has been led astray needs a push in the right direction. A person who lacks love in life craves unconditional love no human is capable of. Eventually, we all start to yearn for something stronger—something more substantial than a sign.

I was so bitter with hatred that I had no place in my heart for love—not even for God. When you have experienced years of trauma, have been betrayed by almost everyone you love, and lost all those whom you cared about to misfortune, prayers, and miracles seem foolish. Every positive emotion starts to get on your nerves when there's not an ounce of positivity in your life. What's the point of loving when love gets snatched from you? It's hard for you to believe that someone you can't even see could love you so much that he would give his only begotten son so that you could have life and have it abundantly.

After fighting my faith for so long, I was so hurt, desperate, and broken I had no other choice but to surrender my life completely to God. I couldn't fight it anymore because I had no alternative. I couldn't latch on to my pride, hurt, or stubbornness because I needed God's help more than anything. I am a living, breathing example and hope for those who have given up on their beliefs after years of disappointments. I am here to tell you today that if you keep

RISE IN PURPOSE

praying and keep believing, God will show up and show out in your life. Just give in instead of holding back. Once you surrender to God, you'll get clarity in life. You won't have to ruminate, overthink, or worry unnecessarily because the answers will start appearing right before your eyes.

Trusting God was very hard for me, and sometimes, it still is. After all these years, I still struggle with my faith. You may form a connection with God based on fleeting desperation, but maintaining it is a lifelong process. I know for a fact if you spend some time alone with Him, meditating on His word and allowing Him to speak to you, it will become easier. When you keep trying, you start to see the results of your efforts. You'll start to feel His love flow through you. The closer you are to God, the closer He will be to you. Like every relationship, your bond with God requires effort on your part. You can't just expect to get anything your heart desires without praying for it. You just have to establish a connection through prayer, and He will respond.

Losing someone close to you in a sudden and traumatic event causes you to become fearful. You start to grow apprehensive about praying in fear of having your expectations shattered. Every time you start to pray, your heart is filled with doubt because your prayers were never answered in the first place. A mother tries her best to shelter her children from any harm since their birth. The fear of losing a child is a feeling that always prevails in a mother's heart, no matter how old they get. The thoughts of their child's safety always remain in the back of their minds. Because of Grant's death, I was forced to face this fear head-on. Often, this dread and uncertainty hold a grip on survivors' hearts—a grip they can never escape. This fear keeps haunting you, plaguing your mind. These terrifying thoughts start to take over your faith.

Many people never find their way back, but I am blessed to have survived this trauma. Many people struggle all their lives to heal their wounds and move past those terrifying experiences. I was afraid of everything when my relationship with God began. I couldn't bring myself to entertain the hope of recovery after what I had gone through. When I first started walking on the nature trail, I was terrified of people, my future, my past, and everything else you can think of. Every time someone looked my way, I had the urge to recoil—to withdraw into myself. Whenever someone talked to me, I found myself at a loss for words. Every time someone mentioned my past, I found myself triggered. The fear of uncertainty and endless possibilities kept me confined to my comfort zone whenever I tried to pave my path forward.

Before Christ saved me, my mind was plagued with anxiety, depression, anger, and confusion. In my helplessness, I knew there was no hope of recovery for me. No therapy, self-help book, or positive anecdotes brought me peace of mind or happiness. I knew I was going to die soon—either of a natural cause or due to my self-destructive habits. Most days, I was barely conscious enough to eat or drink properly. My body had become frail with the lack of nutrition, and my health was only deteriorating due to alcohol consumption.

When I was at the height of despair, Jesus told me, "If I was going to take your life, I would have done it while you were living in the home that I relocated you from, I need for you to trust me. I have given you authority to trample on snakes and scorpions and to overcome all the power of the enemy; nothing will harm you." (Luke 10:19)

When I read that verse, I didn't recognize it from the Bible. It didn't click that Jesus was speaking to me with these signs until a friend of mine texted the verse out of the blue. I realized I didn't have to be a bible scholar or a saint to seek God's help. It didn't matter if I wasn't perfect or didn't have my life in order because God taught me how to seek guidance from the Bible.

As I grew closer to God, I found out that being fearful was perfectly fine as long as you don't allow it to debilitate you or stop you from following through with the plans He has for you. Consider yourself wise to fear God because most people don't and end up heading for destruction. Having a fear of God keeps you in alignment with His will for your life. These feelings are only a stepping stone in your recovery.

When fear adds to the storm of all the negative emotions, it might seem unfair to you. After enduring so much, you want to be led gently with love. You crave words of reaffirmation rather than dreadful admonishment, but just as a parent uses strict measures to discipline you, so does God. Don't lose faith in God because you're suffering; it will only lead to regrets.

God loves us so much that when we are weak, he is strong, and his plans are always greater than ours. When you feel like you can't see any rhyme or reason for your sufferings, I advise you to turn to God for every detail of your day. Change your life, and follow the wisdom of the Bible to bring yourself back on track. Try your best to believe that what He is telling you is in your best interest.

Chapter 10
Forgiveness

"Get rid of all bitterness, rage, anger, harsh words, and slander, as well as all types of evil behavior. Instead, be kind to each other, tenderhearted, forgiving one another, just as God, through Christ, has forgiven you."

(Ephesians 4:31)

"And forgive us our debts, as we also have forgiven our debtors."

(Matthew 6:12)

"Do not judge, and you will not be judged. Do not condemn, and you will not be condemned. Forgive, and you will be forgiven."

(Luke 6:37)

When feelings of resentment continuously build in hearts, no force is strong enough to keep evil from breeding. The seed may be sown as a feeling of self-pity or victim mentality. However, eventually, it takes root and develops into spitefulness. It all stems from despair, the haunting lack of purpose, the utter loss of hope, and the cursing blindness to blessings that trap us in a void. When we feel lost, there's no one we can trust and no one we can open up to. We exist painfully alone in this world. Besides meaningless indulgence, nothing accompanies us in the void until the agony of our pointless existence gives birth to resentment. Once this resentment is left unchecked, nothing but evil forces of hatred and vengeance help us hold on to life. We abandon love, positivity, and hope. Nothing but resentment drives us forward in life.

It can be the most challenging thing to let go of it. Eventually, we become attached to this destructive way of life. Leading a stable, happy life seems impossible. When there's no hope in life, only the intensity of our hatred sustains us. It takes over our desire to live a normal life and dictates that we become the worst version of ourselves. The negative voice in our head takes over our lives. All our decisions are ruled by this feeling of resentment. Instead of making progress and working on ourselves, we give up on not only ourselves but also those who love us. We abandon our relationships and push people away.

Clawing our way out of this meaningless existence seems next to impossible. When you build a home in darkness, you grow addicted to this endless cycle of pain. Stepping out of your comfort zone and putting in some effort is far more challenging than slowly deteriorating into nothingness. There's nothing more tragic than lost potential, a life lost without realizing its purpose. We forget this simple truth when we're lost in this overwhelming darkness. Living in the moment, we stop envisioning our future in the long run. These emotions blind us to the extent that we do not think twice while destroying our lives.

I'm done faking smiles. I'm done enduring. I'm done putting on a brave face. I don't care about anything anymore. What's the point of all this suffering? What have I done to deserve this hell? As I would mull over these resentful thoughts, no reward or promise of heaven seemed enough to make up for the excruciating battles of life. After all the suffering I had gone through, I felt like God hated me. Since my childhood, I have only seen sufferings in life. No matter how hard I tried to remind myself of my golden days with my children, the cruelty of fate was too overpowering. No matter how hard I tried to feel grateful for my blessings, there was too much suffering. I could not see past the pain I was experiencing.

My struggle with forgiveness was a journey. No matter how hard I tried to find it within myself to forgive and move on, the thought was incomprehensible. I didn't find peace overnight, and it certainly wasn't easy or straightforward. Every night, I felt an overwhelming rage. My hatred was so strong I could barely contain it. I wanted to seek revenge, demand justice, or burn everything down if I couldn't have Grant back. How do you forgive the murderer of your child? How do you find peace when the restlessness of vengeance keeps you up all night?

Most of the time, we can't even let go of a petty, snarky remark. Many people struggle to forgive an unintended or harmless mistake. They hold grudges over a person's moment of weakness. People keep scores, biding their time to get back at each other for mistakes that should be long forgotten. They break family ties over something insignificant. They end long-term relationships in the heat of the moment. Forgiving the monstrosity of your child's ruthless murder would seem incomprehensible to any sane mind, but I did it, and I made it through.

If God could help me forgive those who murdered my kid for nothing, he can do *anything*. It's nothing short of a miracle. Although it may not seem like a big deal to everyone, it felt impossible to me. I mean, I was helpless and desperate. What could I do? We can carry those feelings of hatred for so long. Eventually, we have to move forward in life. When I look back, I didn't even want to entertain the thought of forgiveness, much less of moving on. When someone would try to help me, I would lash out. How dare they suggest something so outrageous? They couldn't understand the depths of my pain. Whenever someone suggested it to me, I would turn my face away in disgust, my eyes would flash with red-hot rage, and coldness would seep through my chest.

"I can't even imagine it!" I would spit out the words with hatred. No words are enough to explain the anger I felt. Even if I tried to communicate, they couldn't understand. I couldn't reach out to anyone in the world.

RISE IN PURPOSE

Sitting among friends and family, I realized their meaningless chatter would frustrate me. Their small talk frustrated me to no end. Why would I care to know if my friend found an amazing handbag on sale or what my neighbor did over the weekend? I felt sickened by the mundanity of this world. When I tried to find something to occupy my mind with, I would find myself staring off into space. When I tried to fill my time with something, I lost interest in activities within minutes. I just wanted to be left alone with my thoughts. I just wanted Grant back, and nothing or nobody could change that.

One incident particularly signifies the extreme hatred I felt. It captures the intensity of resentment I felt over the injustice my son experienced. After the police caught the kids who took Grant's life, it was all over the news. Every time I heard those headlines, my blood boiled with rage. I could only see red. My heart filled with sorrow over the helplessness I felt. I recall journalists and news reporters constantly approaching me with questions I neither wanted to respond to nor knew how to. Sometimes, I wanted to yell into their microphones and express my rage at the world, but I kept my silence. However, after constant nagging from their end, during one of the news interviews, I didn't hesitate to speak my mind.

The reporter asked me, "Ma'am, would you be willing to forgive these kids?" He put out the question so nonchalantly that I couldn't believe my ears. It was a ridiculous question, to begin with. Who asks such a question to a grieving mother? Who is inconsiderate and heartless enough to entertain such a thought?

"Forgive them?" I asked incredulously. I was already shaking with rage. The reporter backed off nervously at the display of my emotions. "JESUS FORGIVES! I DON'T!" I yelled back at the top of my lungs. I wanted to continue screaming until my throat would go raw. I wanted to let out all the anguish of sleepless nights, purposeless days, and meaningless existence. I wanted those kids to see me and know the consequences of their actions. I wanted them to suffer just as much as I did. I wanted my anguish to fill their minds with dread and remorse and keep them from having a night of peaceful sleep.

While I burned with rage, the reporter and the cameraman looked at each other and started to laugh hysterically. I couldn't care less; they were laughing at me. It didn't matter if the whole world saw my reaction or if they watched me in a moment of extreme vulnerability. I didn't care if I became a laughing stock before the world as a whole. I didn't care if my grief became a topic of their conversation. Obviously, I didn't think anything about my reaction was funny at the time, but now I laugh when I think about it.

Though I yearned for some peace of mind, I didn't want to forgive them. Not just because I couldn't bring myself to but also because I felt like I was failing Grant. How could I

RISE IN PURPOSE

get justice for my son if I forgave his murderers? How could I live with myself if I allowed myself to heal? Mourning helped me deal with the overwhelming guilt. Although a part of me wanted to let go, I felt like I'd be betraying my son. The feelings of happiness filled my heart with shame. Due to my guilt, I held on to those negative feelings even if they held me back from healing.

God showed me that I was heading for destruction by holding on to all that anger and my self-sabotaging behaviors. It took a while, but gradually, I started to escape that darkness. Eventually, I started to counter those negative thoughts and started paving the way toward light. How could my son approve of this destruction when he loved me at my worst? How could he stand to watch me kill myself slowly when God hadn't decided it was my time? I wasn't failing Grant by holding on to him but by giving up on myself.

Once I accepted this truth, I became far more receptive to getting help. I started opening myself up to love and positive experiences. When my faith was rekindled, I realized there was a purpose behind all of the pain. No one but God can give you life or take it from you. If only He held that power, then how could I keep cursing some misguided souls? Although I still felt sorrow for my tragedy, I decided to let go of everything that held me back. I questioned God how he could let something so traumatizing happen to me, but I started counting my blessings to see His love. If he could give me a beautiful son and daughter, then he must have been taken away from me for a purpose.

You may not understand this then, but I promise you that if you ask him in prayer, he will reveal it to you. If you hold on to your faith, you'll watch miracles unfold before your eyes. I prayed without ceasing, asking God to help me forgive those kids and their families. I also prayed and asked God to turn their hearts toward him. Believe me, when the seed of forgiveness blossomed in my heart, it was nothing short of a miracle. If you are struggling with unforgiveness, I understand exactly how you feel, and I can assure you that if you give in to God and ask Him to help you, He will.

Chapter 11
Prayer

"If my people who are called by my name humble themselves, and pray and seek my face and turn from their wicked ways, then I will hear from heaven and will forgive their sin and heal their land."

(2 Chronicles 7:14)

"You can ask for anything in my name, and I will do it so that the son can bring glory to the father."

(John 14:13)

"Do not be anxious about anything, but in every situation, by prayer and petition, with thanksgiving, present your requests to God."

(Philippians 4:6)

There is a bigger purpose to life than career, family, and friends; it is to please God by praying to him. Before any other role we might assume in life, it is our responsibility to thank our creator. It is necessary to express our gratitude toward Him through our actions and prayers. No matter what you do in life, you are to strive to bring glory to God. That means your prayers should bring glory to him and his purpose for your life. Your words and actions should be reflective of your love for God.

DONESE K. GORDON

Unfortunately, most people forget this purpose and indulge in worldly things. They forego their spiritual responsibilities in favor of materialistic gains. They prioritize making money, putting up a show, and living recklessly over seeking the truth of life. For them, waking up early for work is more important than waking up early to pray. They spend their entire lives like mindless zombies, abiding by a bunch of rules without ever realizing their own true potential. I myself had been this way for most of my life. I never stopped to think about the meaning of existence. Like everyone else, I went through the same mindless, mundane routine every day. I let life pass me by without ever wondering why I was put in this world—what God could've wanted from me.

I would pray generic prayers in my head at night and even skipped those much of the time. I only remembered to seek God when I needed to—when I was desperate and could find no way out of the situations I landed myself in. I always went to God when I needed something, such as a financial need, protection from something, or gaining material possessions. My love for God was just as selfish and self-absorbed as the love we feel for human beings. I only cared for my own well-being and forgot my moral responsibility toward God the moment I acquired what I had been praying for. No matter how selfish my own love was, I yearned for the kind of unconditional love only God could give me. Prayer became secondary to me because of all the other distractions in my life.

RISE IN PURPOSE

It's difficult to maintain a spiritual life in a fast-paced world like ours. Every moment of our day is spent worrying about the next necessary task. We don't get a moment to spare for our well-being, for our mental health, or for the nurture of our souls. There's so much to do in such little time, but somehow, we always focus on achieving material things and completely skip remembering God. We refuse to set our priorities right because temporary gain seems more urgent and necessary than our long-term betterment. Instead of thinking things through, we seek instant gratification. Before I had realized my true purpose and grounded myself, I never paused to think about those things. I never envisioned where I was heading. Only the current circumstances mattered. Every day, I would wake up in the morning, pick up my phone, and hop on social media before thanking God for giving me a new day to live. Checking notifications and the likes on my posts seemed far more important.

We often think we are praying enough, but that's not the case. Just saying the words is not enough. Just asking for what we want is not enough, either. The truth is, most of us spend hours praying, but we don't ask God for enough. God can give us everything, but we have to keep faith. It is important to break down in front of the Lord and show Him all the burdens of your heart.

Without being vulnerable before God, how can we expect to have our prayers answered? If our prayers are half-hearted, how can we expect to get heard? If we refuse to put our trust in God, how can we expect God to listen to us? We have to remove all barriers of unnecessary worries, shed off all layers of pride, and let go of our greed and resentment. When we ask God with a pure heart out of sheer desperate love, God rewards us by giving us everything we have ever wanted.

I didn't know the meaning of prayer or the correct way to pray to God, so I continued to neglect it for the longest time. It didn't take priority in my life—not until my son lost his life. My entire world was shaken. When the responsibilities of life seemed secondary, I could finally begin to see what took precedence in life. I could finally see the ugly truth of this world. Every single thing in this world is temporary, besides the love we carry in our spirits. When I realized how insignificant the world and its things were, I decided to set things right. I became cautious with how I spent my time. Everything in this world disintegrates in just a blink of an eye and disappears from the face of the earth like it never existed.

No friends, family, job, or material things could bring my son back to me or give me the peace I needed to cope with the loss. Every moment of satisfaction or happiness was fleeting. It all quickly passed by and was followed by an overwhelming sense of hollowness. No number of empty praises or meaningless luxuries could fill the void in my chest. It was God and His remembrance that made me realize the importance of spiritual connection. Once I

RISE IN PURPOSE

started establishing my connection with God, I started feeling a sense of fulfillment. I stopped feeling the need to rely on these temporary moments of bliss because I had finally found eternal peace of mind.

Prayer is a plea to God. It is a means to establish communication with him. In order to move smoothly into the world, we need God's help and His spirit to work for us as a guide. It is impossible to achieve anything in this world without God's guidance. Throughout our lives, we meet many people who betray us and try to sabotage our success. Despite all our hard work, we can't protect ourselves from what this world might throw at us. Only God can protect and guide us from the malevolent forces of the world. The only way we can build a spiritual connection with God is if we admit our helplessness before Him. It is important to maintain humility while praying to God, but it is more important to know what to ask Him for when we pray. We only walk blindly in the darkness without knowing what to ask.

I didn't know how to pray properly at first. I didn't even know what I wanted because I didn't value myself enough. However, Jesus taught me how to be a prayer warrior. He showed me, or rather, took me by the hand and guided me through the turmoil I had been going through. Whenever I felt lost, he showed me the path I was meant to take. I went to him humbly, and he put me on the right path.

When I started to pray about certain things, my entire life changed before my eyes. I gave myself up to Jesus and stopped worrying about where I was headed. Now, as soon as my feet hit the floor in the mornings, I get straight on my knees to pray and thank God for waking me up and allowing me to see another day. My mornings started with Jesus, and I continued to seek him throughout the day. That's how my relationship was originally established through prayer.

Prayer in the name of Jesus is not a blank check to get whatever you want in life. Of course, you can't ask to become a millionaire before bed and find a check on the kitchen counter the next morning. It is a humble and heartfelt way to present your request to God and to trust him to answer you as long as you pray according to his will. It is necessary to believe that He knows best. If your prayers don't get answered, there must be a reason. If you ask and do not receive, it is not in the will of God for your life. Maybe He has something better in store for you, or maybe it is a way for you to keep returning to Him.

God invites you to be persistent in your prayers. He will delay your requests, sometimes while humbling you and teaching you about patience. There will be times when you will not have the strength to pray; however, you have to pray without ceasing until the Holy Spirit tells you to stop. Stay connected with your faith, no matter what happens. Eventually, you'll start to see the light at the end of the tunnel. Pray when you are worried, anxious, fearful, afraid, happy, sad, insecure, mad, bitter, angry, etc. The key to a successful relationship with God is through prayer and thanksgiving.

I can't stress this enough: if God does not answer your prayer, continue to be thankful because an unanswered prayer is a blessing in disguise. You may not be able to see it at the time, but it's true. God is aware of all of our needs before we even ask for them. He cares about us and knows the burdens residing in our hearts, but he loves to see us sit in front of him and vocalize our struggles.

"The eyes of the Lord are toward the righteous and his ears toward their cry."

(Psalms 34:15)

Sometimes, the answer to our prayers is yes; sometimes, it is no, and sometimes, he chooses to answer in a different way. We might not see the answer as a simple yes because it doesn't happen right away. Indeed, God sees the bigger picture and knows that if what we are asking for isn't good for us, he will deny the plea and provide us with something better, something we haven't even asked for. Sometimes, the answer may come in the form of waiting. Although it might seem irritating, this waiting has value. Just stay patient, keep praying, and stay connected to God.

We pray, "Let your Kingdom come, let your will be done on earth as it is in heaven." (Matthew 6:10)

When we say this, we are praying for access to the kingdom of God in our lives. God runs his Kingdom and is in charge, not man.

Jesus said, "For indeed, the kingdom of God is within you." (Luke 17:21). Here, He was speaking of himself, not of this World. It is not religious rules and regulations but "righteousness and peace and joy in the Holy Spirit." (Romans 14:17)

Through prayer, Jesus will lead and guide you into your purpose while transforming you from the inside out. You will not only become free to be the person God created you to be, but you will also be transformed into a new person and have supernatural powers to do anything you set your mind to.

A part of your purpose is for the advancement of God's Kingdom on earth, and he promises us while doing so, he will bless us with the desires of your heart, not what you want but what you need. God knows what you need in order to be happy, so give your heart and all of your plans to him and be open to the things that he blesses you with.

There are many things in this world that are beyond human comprehension. There is a reason why some people accept the answers to their pleas faster than others or why some have been spared from misery and pain while others suffer at every point of their lives. God works in mysterious ways, as we have all heard. So, we should trust in his process and keep falling to our knees to pray.

RISE IN PURPOSE

Chapter 12
Purpose

"The son of man did not come to be served but to serve."

(Matthew 20:28)

"Write the vision and make it plain so that he who reads it may run with it."

(Habakkuk 2:2)

"And we know that all things work together for good to them that love God, to them who are the called according to his purpose."

(Romans 8:28)

When we're going through something difficult, we tend to become short-sighted. We feel so bitter about the injustice of our circumstances that we refuse to see a silver lining behind things. I did not know it at the time, but God revealed to me that he was using Grant's death as a part of his plan for my salvation. This tragedy was just another means of pushing me into greatness. I was in so much pain that I refused to accept my cursed reality. I started to question God, asking him, "Why am I here? What happens to you after you die? Are you really real? Who is Jesus? Why am I going through this? What is the purpose of life?"

DONESE K. GORDON

All of us have to deal with these existential questions at some point in life. All of us wonder about the purpose behind our existence. But the simple answer regarding the purpose of life is God created humankind for His glory, and the ultimate purpose of existing in the world is to glorify Him. Humans have been put in this world to serve God, to worship Him, and to love him with our entire beings.

"Serve the Lord with gladness! Come into his presence with singing! Know that the Lord, he is God! It is he who made us, and we are his; we are his people, and the sheep of his pasture."

(Psalms 100:2–3)

We spend our entire lives trying to find our true purpose. We try different things in life, hoping something will bring us some peace of mind. We all have a deep yearning in our souls to achieve something great in life. We don't feel satisfied unless we make a difference or make an impact. Some people find their true calling in their passion, while others want to help the poor and needy. No matter what you decide to do in life, there's only one reason we are put on this earth—to worship God. It is through our acts of servitude and prayer that we fulfill this true purpose in life.

We can fulfill our purpose only by glorifying God and by being faithful to him. If we remain faithful to God, we will start to understand the path we're supposed to walk on in life. It is only then that we will achieve a greater place in heaven after dying. All of this knowledge came to me way later in life. Before I understood this truth, I was always trying to make sense of my sufferings. After understanding why I had to endure so much, I stopped complaining about my problems. I never cared about life after death because I never had a relationship with God.

After losing someone, we tend to think about life after death constantly. We constantly wonder if there's a parallel universe out there where the souls of your loved ones might exist. I never knew anyone who died and came back to life to talk about it, so what difference did my prayers and my glorifying make? No one really knows for sure what happens to our souls after we die. Little did I know, I was heading for the biggest fight of my life: the battle between the enemy and God for my soul. My soul left when Grant did, but Jesus brought me back. The day Grant died, I felt like I had no reason to continue living. Most days, I felt like I continued to breathe, but there was no sign of life in me. The things I previously found enjoyable; I couldn't care less about them. I didn't care about my health or entertainment. Although I was alive, I might as well have just died.

I felt so enraged at losing Grant; I couldn't understand why I had to go through something so excruciatingly painful. It was beyond my understanding why my beloved son had to die at such a young age. God explained to me that Grant's time here on earth was up anyway. I often cursed myself for not being able to prevent Grant's death. There was nothing I could have done to prevent his death or change it. No one can give you life or take it from you but Him, and if He allowed it to happen, it happened for a bigger purpose. I started to understand this truth a lot later in life. The real journey starts after death, and Grant is in a better world now. It took me a long time to really start believing this, but I eventually came to terms with his death. I believe this to be true because God has pulled me closer to Him, and I have felt things I could never imagine.

Initially, I couldn't understand why God allowed Satan to take Grant from me after I had already suffered so much all my life. I know he had his reasons to take Grant from me, even after how he went away from this world. His loss had made me hopeless, but as I made a connection with God, I found my purpose in life. It didn't matter how much suffering I had to endure. In the end, only one thing mattered—my love for God. It was to create a strong relationship with the Lord, one that promises communion with him after death.

Your relationship with God, along with your mission statement, is your life's purpose. The answers to the questions "Why was I born, and what did God create me to do during my time here on earth?" can only be answered by God. Oftentimes, we can't decide what to do with our time here on earth. We feel like we are wasting our lives. In order for you to live the life God created for you, you have to know

RISE IN PURPOSE

the answer to those questions. God will answer the questions for you when you ask him in prayer. The answers will start appearing before you as your fate unfolds before your eyes.

You will be surprised what great plans he has in store for you, trust me. You just have to stay patient and keep faith in God. I worked in the staffing industry for years as an Independent Executive Recruiter, placing adults in careers. I was very successful in the beginning at building a company, marketing, and helping people gain employment. However, when you mix money with immaturity, lack of wisdom, addiction, low self-esteem, no discipline, and no self-control, it is a recipe for failure. I started and failed so many times I lost count, but that was before I gave God control of my life. Despite all my failures, I trusted God to turn things around for me.

When you develop a relationship with God, you also develop trust in him. Despite all the hurdles you face, you start to have faith. You believe everything will be okay, even if everything is falling apart in your life. There comes a natural calmness in your personality as you decide to give Him control of your life. You start to realize there's no point in worrying unnecessarily because God has already decided your fate. He has created us in His image and knows what's best for us. So, if He knows our needs and is aware of our miseries, then why do we hesitate to trust Him?

When we try to take control of our lives, we experience physical, emotional, and spiritual fatigue. There's nothing in this world that can go against God's will, so why do we spend so much time worrying? We aren't sent into this world to deal with all the burdens alone. We are supposed to rely on God whenever we are met with difficulties in life. God has designed our natures to lean and depend on Him whenever necessary. If you allow God to help you, He will turn that failure into a lesson and a lesson into a blessing. You'll start to feel grateful for all the tests of endurance you have been put through in life.

Trusting God means loving Him more every day. It means hoping for the best even when you're faced with the worst fate possible. It is hard to trust Him, especially when life is testing you. Most of us are afraid to let go because we are so used to being in control that giving the wheel of our life to someone else seems scary. Letting go can be incredibly scary because we don't know what the future might hold for us. The only way you can achieve peace and contentment is by having complete faith in the entity of God.

God was using my failures, along with Grant's passing, to teach me and prepare me for my purpose. Before Grant passed, he came into my office and asked, "Did you work on your staffing company today?" He seemed to be expecting a positive response, so my response must have disappointed him.

RISE IN PURPOSE

"No," I responded honestly, and he looked at me with a bizarre look. For a moment, he shook his head, but then he nodded understandingly.

"Okay," he said, taking a step closer to my desk. "I am going to help you with your staffing company."

I laughed. I felt guilty that my son had to feel responsible for helping me with my work. "No, you can't. You have to attend college when you graduate from high school."

"Okay then, I am going to help you on the weekends. You need me to help you, and I'm going to help you succeed, I promise," he replied calmly. I felt incredibly grateful for having such a loving and understanding son.

I didn't pay much attention to the conversation back then, but later on, I realized that it was God speaking through my son. It was his voice that was supporting me through my work. He was going to be my angel, helping me with my purpose. I often reminisce about that day and wish I'd paid more attention to my son and his innocent attempt to save me from the struggle I had been going through with the company. But it wasn't too late.

Although Grant was gone, I had found a way to peacefully cope with the loss, as well as create a strong connection with God. Once I came to terms with my loss, everything started to make sense to me. By doing so, I found my purpose. I birthed Grant's World through it all, which pushed me to my purpose. The tragic loss of my son led me to find my true calling in life. I now help adults and youth with employment opportunities and resources.

Grant had finally helped me with my company. Eventually, things started to take a turn for the better. Though I would have wanted him to see my journey toward God, I am glad to know that I will have eternal life with him. Without the suffering that fate had put me through, I would never have realized my purpose.

Chapter 13
Addictions

"No temptation has overtaken you except what is common to mankind. And God is faithful, he will not let you be tempted beyond what you can bear. But when tempted he will always provide a way out so that you can endure it."

(1 Corinthians 10:13)

"And do not get drunk with wine, for that is debauchery, but be filled with the Spirit."

(Ephesians 5:18)

"Nor thieves, nor the covetous, nor drunkards, nor revilers, nor extortioners shall inherit the Kingdom of God."

(1 Corinthians 6:10)

When we're lost in the darkness of despair, nothing worsens our condition more than addictions. Our addictions grip our hearts, clutch our minds, and drive us toward evil until there's no way back. When we're grieving, it's an incredibly dangerous path to walk on. Once you're lost, there's no way back. Try as you might; you'll only be pulled deeper into the darkness until a tragedy strikes— until a life is lost in vain. No matter how perilous it is, we always tend to seek addictions to numb the pain. Due to our impulsivity, we overlook the consequences. Our rage and grief blind us to the extent we forget our own value. We forget there's a purpose to our existence and there's value to our life.

Once you discover your purpose, it is imperative that you follow Christ closely as he orders your steps. There is no way you can accomplish the plans he has for you with addictions to anything outside of God. When your ability to reason is compromised, it is impossible to head straight on the right path. There are so many voices in our heads you don't know which one to follow. You stumble around in the darkness, trying to figure out your way, but you feel pulled in every direction. Mind-altering substances really drown out the voice of God and will have you following all the wrong voices.

You want your thoughts to be in alignment with God's will for your life. Even though his thoughts are greater than ours, you want yours not to be far from his. When your thoughts are disoriented, you start to feel lost. You lose faith in life, start questioning your existence, and lead life meaninglessly. I had to learn this the hard way, but it taught me that anything outside of God's presence was temporary gratification, a false sense of self, and it brought no peace. In fact, it completely destroys our peace of mind.

I knew I needed to stop drinking. It was destroying my mind, my body, and my soul. I had completely given up control. However, I continued to do so due to my lack of wisdom and understanding of God's word, and Grant's

RISE IN PURPOSE

letter proved just how bad it was. The people I was around did not make it any better. The lack of support and isolation only worsened my addictions. When Christ started the process of freeing me from bondage, my fiancé informed me that he was leaving. I felt shocked—betrayed even. I just couldn't bring myself to believe I was being abandoned once again after everything I had lost. His reason was that he could not get any peace because of my drinking.

Everyone, including his family, acted like I was delusional, and Grant's death had taken a toll on my mind. Even if I tried to change my habits, no one was willing to trust me. I was devastated and started praying to God like never before. I prayed for him to fix our relationship and free me from my addictions. At the time, my relationship with my fiancé was the most important part of my life. However, before my prayers were answered, God revealed the true colors of my fiancé.

The day before he left, I found drugs on my bathroom counter. I can't thank God enough for the gift of exposure. While my fiancé demonized and demeaned me for an addiction I couldn't help, he was struggling with an addiction of his own. God showed me that the reason my fiancé could not get any peace was because he had relapsed on drugs.

He didn't leave me. I felt so relieved that I wasn't dropped and discarded once again. God removed him so that He could answer my prayers and set me free. I felt so ashamed because everyone except for me knew he had a severe drug problem. I was grieving Grant and battling my own demons, so I never cared about his. I never realized he could be dealing with the same problem. At the time, I realized I was so much in my own head I didn't realize what was happening in anyone else's life—not even my fiancé's. I told my cousin what happened, and she looked at me and said, "You are tripping. The whole world is on drugs, alcohol, or something. You are so weak!"

The blunt words hurt me. *What did she know about my problems?* She couldn't even begin to imagine how hard I had to fight every single day. I was so insulted by the fact that she called me weak that I stopped drinking for a short period of time. I remained adamant about staying sober until a friend of mine shared with me that God told her I could start drinking again in the future, but I had to heal first. I knew that already, but it was easier said than done. Disclaimer: He removed both of them from my life.

From that day forward, I started to doubt what Jesus had spoken to me. *She must be right*; I would tell myself when I would feel my will wavering. *I mean, Jesus allowed the disciples to drink wine in the Bible, so it's okay; I can stop when I feel like it.* I started drinking again, wine occasionally. Then, occasionally, it turned into daily, and before I knew it, I was severely depressed. Although I knew what I was doing was bad for me, I couldn't control myself. I continued lying to myself. I continued consuming alcohol even if it was ruining my life.

RISE IN PURPOSE

I cried out to God in prayer one day. I was distressed at my condition. I couldn't understand why God led me back to it. When I questioned God, the spirit led me to walk on the trail. He spoke to me and said, "I love you, and don't be mad at me. I led you back to it so you will know not to touch it ever again. Alcohol is a depressant, and it will destroy you and your purpose." He then led me to a Bible verse that said, "What good is a man to gain the whole world and lose his soul."

Once I started listening to God, I started recovering. I started getting a hold of my senses. Eventually, I got enough control to give it up entirely. I have not touched another drop of alcohol since and never will. The truth is wine represents grape juice in the Bible. However, man fermented it into alcohol. The fermented wine is what Jesus warns us to stay away from because it alters your ability to think, and it can become an idol in your lives. Obviously, not everyone sees it that way. Not everyone thinks that alcohol drives them from the right path. However, once you stop consuming alcohol permanently, you'll start to see many positive changes in your life.

I was addicted to alcohol, tobacco, prescription medications, social media, negative news, gossiping, compulsive shopping, abusive relationships, and self-sabotaging behaviors. Jesus freed me from all of those addictions, and He can free you, too. Ask God through prayer to free you from ALL addictions and to strengthen your mind. There's nothing that strengthens your mind more than faith. Once you let yourself go, you stop worrying unnecessarily. You stop caring what the world thinks because you have God by your side. When you don't feel alone, weak, helpless, or afraid, you don't have to rely on mind-numbing substances to cope. Faith brings you the inner peace you have been yearning for all along.

You may have addictions that you don't even realize. Anything you pursue obsessively in an unhealthy way can turn into an addiction. Withdrawing from an addiction can be intensely painful. It disorients your perspective and turns your world upside down. When you're pulling away, you might have a lot of doubts and uncertainties. The void that you had previously been filling with addictions only feels bigger. You start to feel it more intensely than before. You have to fight those addictions with every fiber of your being. When the fight is over, you either give in and revert back to your unhealthy habits or emerge victorious, stronger than before.

Believe me, the struggle is worth it. Once you get back in control, the world appears so much brighter, the colors look so much more vibrant, and your vision is broadened. You start to see things from a different perspective. When you start to appreciate the beauty of nature, your heart fills with gratitude toward God. All the things that previously confused you start to make sense. It all perfectly aligns with why you had to suffer the way you did; the grand

RISE IN PURPOSE

scheme of life is revealed to you. Sufferings no longer agonize you; injustice doesn't enrage you, and failures don't make you bitter and resentful. Every failure starts to look like a lesson—a glimmer of hope for a better future.

Chapter 14
Fruits of the Spirit

"Now the works of the flesh are evident, which are: adultery, fornication, uncleanness, lewdness, idolatry, sorcery, hatred, contentions, jealousies, outbursts of wrath, selfish ambitions, dissensions, heresies, envy, murders, drunkenness, revelries, and the like; of which I tell you beforehand, just as I also told you in time past, that those who practice such things will not inherit the kingdom of God. But the fruit of the spirit is love, joy, peace, patience, kindness, goodness, faithfulness, gentleness, and self-control. Against such there is no law."

(Galatians 5:19-23)

You must be born again to inherit the Kingdom of God on earth. You must leave behind your old self, change your bad habits, and transform yourself into someone following the will of God. The Kingdom of God is your inheritance, and it consists of success, power, peace, joy, righteousness, and the Holy Spirit. Once you start walking on the path of righteousness, you start to reap its benefits. You no longer live according to your old self, which is ruled by its lust of the flesh, impatience, pride, lack of self-control, and lack of discipline. You start to see how that life of depravity has ruined you. All of these things are a hindrance to your success and will stop you from accessing God's Kingdom and the promises He has for your life.

RISE IN PURPOSE

You have to pray and make a conscious decision to become a better version of yourself in all areas of your life, including your character. This kind of change doesn't take place overnight. Every day, you might feel like giving up, but you have to pull yourself together and keep trying. Some days, you struggle to stay consistent. Some days, you feel like all your efforts have been in vain. However, it requires faith and resilience to keep working on yourself, even when you can't always see hope. God cannot fix your counterfeit self, and changing from your old sinful self takes prayer, vulnerability, effort, and lessons from God.

Let me share with you a lesson: God used to teach me patience and perseverance. There are several lessons hidden in unexpected encounters. It depends on us whether we interpret them correctly or wallow in self-pity. Once I got a message from God, I eagerly waited for the events to unfold in my favor. I was at home one day, and God spoke to me clearly and said, "I am about to introduce you to your Kingdom Husband. You do not have to go looking for him. I am going to send him to you." This was unexpected, so the message left me perplexed, but I did as I was told.

A couple of weeks later, I held a job fair at my office for youth. However, no youth attended; adults showed up instead. I felt pretty excited about the event, so all thoughts of the strange message from God had escaped my mind. This guy attended the job fair, and we started to talk. Initially, I didn't make anything of the meeting, but I was intrigued, nonetheless. The guy was overqualified for the position, so I was puzzled about why God led him there. To my surprise, the guy also shared my confusion. He also thought there must be a reason behind the fateful encounter.

When I asked God why this guy was introduced into my life, my question was eventually answered. God told me he was the one He sent to me to be my Kingdom Husband. My excitement grew with God's answer. I looked forward to all the possibilities of how our relationship might progress. We had already developed an instant connection. Our first meeting had been quite unexpected as well.

Ironically, the guy mentioned to me that he was going on a fast for ten days to see why God led him there. The information caught me off guard because I was already scheduled to start a fast on that following Monday. It was incredible how both of us had reached the same decision in order to alleviate our confusion. Not to mention, in the Bible, Boaz found Ruth working in her field like myself, so I just knew it was destiny. My future looked so much brighter all of a sudden, and I looked forward to positive, happy days. I was super excited because I was receiving one of my promises from God. I felt incredibly grateful to God for introducing that person into my life.

The guy and I met again after we fasted. The conversation flowed, and we could relate with each other over a lot of things. While we were getting to know one another, he shared with me how he struggled with moving on from a

RISE IN PURPOSE

relationship that he had been in for eleven years. I was struck by this revelation because of the promise from God. Without thinking twice, I jumped into a defensive mode of speaking. I said to him arrogantly, "I am super obedient when it comes to keeping God's commandments. When he tells me to do something, I do it. I know not to look back."

It looked like the guy would retort defensively for a moment, but he calmly said to me instead, "Well, I am not perfect, but thank God for grace."

I felt a little embarrassed for losing my composure, but I didn't dwell on it. We left the restaurant, and I only briefly pondered over my interaction with the guy. Some days after that, God spoke to me and said, "If you see any of your exes from your past, I want you to keep going." I took the message for granted since I thought I had already moved on from my ex. *Why would I pay my ex any attention?* I thought.

Later that day, I was at the car wash, and guess who thought she saw her ex and almost broke her neck, jumping out of the car to run up to him, only to find out it wasn't him? Well, I obviously did that. All previous thoughts escaped my mind. At the moment, I just cared about meeting my ex again. So much for being obedient to God! Once I realized my mistake, I felt embarrassed for my behavior and vowed never to think too highly of myself. God spoke to me and said, "It's not him, but didn't I tell you if you saw him to keep going?"

The next day, my supposed "Kingdom Husband" was to meet me at the office, but he didn't show up or answer any of my text messages. I recalled how our last meeting at the restaurant had gone. I was so confused because I knew this was the man God said was my husband. *Wasn't he meant to be a part of my life? Why is he ignoring me now?* It made no sense to me. *How could someone who was promised to be my husband by God be removed from my life?* Perplexed and dejected, when I questioned God, he told me he had removed the guy from my life. Instead of learning my lesson, I initially listened to my pride. Here came my pride and ego speaking to me; God removed him because he was not obedient to the situation with his ex. This is what I tried to convince myself of.

That wasn't the case. God removed him to teach me three lessons:

1) Don't judge others because we all have fallen short of the glory of God, and it is only by his grace that we are obedient. Nobody is perfect, and everyone is on their own healing journey. We all fall short and fail at times until our faith becomes stronger and we start following God's will.

2) Pride is the quickest way to fall. When you remove your ego and take pride in situations, you can learn the lessons that God is teaching you. Otherwise, you only keep shifting the blame onto others, and you never grow.

RISE IN PURPOSE

3) The final lesson was patience and perseverance. The guy was never intended to be my husband, only a lesson. God will always keep his promises to you. However, he can and will do as he pleases, including changing a person, place, or situation at any time to strengthen your patience and teach you perseverance.

Although I felt a little sad about my shattered hopes, I learned a bigger lesson through the entire ordeal. *What more could I ask for?* In the end, nothing matters more than our bond with ourselves and God. This lesson only strengthened my belief in God. Instead of growing bitter over the broken promise, I learned to surrender to God's will. I could have remained resentful, but I chose to move ahead in life. The experience humbled me, and I never judged anyone else.

Sometimes, we might make huge claims and fail to keep our word. Human beings are full of flaws, and this inconsistency is a part of our life. It is our responsibility to stay humble through our rise and fall. If you've learned to control your impulses, thank God for giving you the strength for it. If you're struggling, then pray to God because only his words and guidance will help you find the discipline you're seeking. Stay patient, stay humble, and don't give up.

Chapter 15
Don't Look Back

"They went out from us, but they did not really belong to us. For if they had belonged to us, they would have remained with us, but their going showed none of them belonged with us."

(1 John 2:19)

"But the LORD hardened Pharaoh's heart and he would not listen to Moses and Aaron, just as the LORD had said to Moses."

(Exodus 9:12)

"But Lot's wife looked back, and she became a pillar of salt."

(Genesis 16:26)

When you're in a toxic environment, it is nearly impossible to grow. All your energy is drained, and you lose sight of your purpose in life. Instead of taking accountability for your actions, you look for ways to shift the blame. You feel like you're stuck in a never-ending cycle, repeating unhealthy patterns, hoping for a change in vain. Oftentimes, self-sabotaging behaviors are the most desperate cry for help. However, this also feeds into the negative cycle of thoughts because it reinforces your unhealthy behavior. It makes you entirely dependent upon another person.

RISE IN PURPOSE

Although it's not wrong to seek support, codependency can often lead to harmful behaviors. As a consequence, it does nothing more than enable you to feed your unhealthy mindset. Truly changing that rigid mindset requires immense effort on your part. In the first place, an unhealthy mindset is a result of years of trauma or a poor way of living. Your mind has been conditioned to think in self-sabotaging ways. Therefore, holding on to faith is a crucial part of positive change.

Earlier, I shared how God removed everyone from my life, with the exception of my daughter. Although she didn't abandon me, God moved her to Texas so she could embark on her own healing journey. Of course, I was devastated. Having already lost my son, I wasn't ready to part with my daughter. At that time, I needed someone by my side more than ever before. When you're suffering, loneliness is the worst thing imaginable. I kept questioning God and blamed myself for things I had no control over. I would often think to myself, *am I so toxic that everyone I love is taken away from me?* He removed family members, friends, associates, and business endeavors from my life. I would cry for hours; it made me despair. Every time I was abandoned, it felt like a punch in my gut. However, it was not my decision who stayed and who left; the decision was God's.

After Grant passed away, I was at the weakest and lowest point of my life. Once I had processed the grief, I had to face the terror of how he lost his life. Murder is so brutal that fear holds you in its steadfast grip until you find a way to escape its clutches. When I learned the severity of the details of his case, I started living in constant fear. I wondered if the people who had harmed him would come after me and my family. I wondered if his friends were hiding something from me, if they knew what happened to him, and were keeping something from me. I constantly read between the lines, trying to find ways to confirm or deny my fears. Sometimes, I felt like I was being lied to without any basis for my convictions. I couldn't bring myself to trust anyone. This paranoia plagued my mind night and day.

Out of desperation, I sought help from God. I asked him to protect me from anything and anybody who wasn't good for me. When your life is plagued by uncertainty, only blind faith can pull you out of that darkness. I had no idea he was going to remove people I considered my friends and family. Initially, it made no sense to me. How could I recover without the emotional support I so desperately needed? How could I have my doubts removed if my fears were just being confirmed? Every abandonment only cemented the fear that had already poisoned my mind.

Eventually, I realized it was God's will and doing. He hardens the hearts of people against you. Once you pray to Him, he will remove anyone or anything that interferes with his purpose for your life. I realized there was a greater reason behind every suffering that I was too ignorant to

RISE IN PURPOSE

understand earlier. It was the reason I was brought into this world, and every hardship pushed me toward that purpose. Of course, coming to terms with this was easier said than done.

People I had known for years, all of a sudden, started calling me weak and pathetic. It was heartbreaking at the time. The brutal words would cut through me, wounding me further; however, now I realize God made me weak on purpose so I could discover my purpose. Those people are no longer in my life, but I remember God assuring me that I will never be ashamed again. When I found the light of faith, I stopped caring what others thought of me. It didn't matter what names they called me because I was on my own healing journey and had found strength in God's words. I knew one day they would regret the way they treated me, so I left it up to God to deal with them.

A couple of months after the pathetic incident, God asked me to buy Christmas gifts for the people he was about to remove from my life. Naturally, I struggled with the task at the time. After how I had been treated, I couldn't help but feel resentful toward those people. However, a part of me still held on to them, hoping against hope to find a way to preserve those relationships. I couldn't even understand if I was hearing my own wishful voice or God's guiding message. When we're yearning for something desperately, we start to see signs leading us toward our desires. Sometimes, we may think the signs are from the universe, guiding us to our true calling; however, it may be nothing but an illusion. So, I asked God for a sign directly instead of overthinking my decision, and God responded.

One day, I was sitting in my car at the bank and needed a pen. The thought occurred to me out of nowhere because I had no need for a pen earlier. Suddenly, I heard the voice of God. He said, "Ask the lady in the car next to you."

I did as I was told and asked her for a pen. There was a message written across the pen. It said, "The LORD said to my Lord, 'Sit at My right hand, till I make Your enemies Your footstool.'" All my doubts started dissipating. I didn't need to worry my mind for answers because I had asked God for guidance directly. I knew it couldn't be a mistake.

That was all the confirmation I needed. So, I obediently dropped the gifts. A sense of calm settled in my chest, and I knew for sure that I was doing the right thing. The glimmer of that lingering hope extinguished. Finally, after hours of futile contemplation, I was ready to let go of the people who no longer served a purpose in my life, and when I was done, God spoke to me again. "Now, walk in your destiny, and don't look back." So, that's what I decided to do.

If you're familiar with the story of Job in the Bible, his friends laughed at him, too, but God blessed him double for his trouble. Don't complain about those who are gone because God can see through people's hearts. It is not our job to see through people's true intentions. We're not

RISE IN PURPOSE

responsible for other people's actions, so it is okay to pull away when they start to hurt you. It's alright to look out for yourself and follow the path God has set out for you. He sees what you can't see, and the sooner you realize this, the easier it becomes to let go of people, places, and things that no longer serve a purpose in your life.

When it is time for you to walk into your purpose, you can't take everybody with you. Not everyone is strong enough to accept their mistakes, humble themselves, and transform themselves for the better. They only stand by your side when it's convenient for them until you eventually outgrow them. Once you realize they're not ready to compromise and make efforts, you have to move on. Some people will not have the ability to handle your walk with Christ. Trying to move forward and shouldering all the burdens of regret will only hinder your progress. You have to accept they were only in your life for a season. Learn the lessons from that relationship, and move forward with life.

I did not understand how critical it was to keep my mouth shut about what God is doing in my life. Because I saw the best in people, I took them at face value. I didn't see a reason to doubt their intentions until I had clear reasons to. I didn't learn my lesson until I was betrayed by a person who I thought was my best friend. God kept telling me to move in silence with this person, and I kept missing the signs because of my lack of understanding.

We often trust others blindly, doubting our own judgments. Of course, I learned my lessons the hard way. I prematurely shared with her the logo I had designed for my business. She copied it for her own business and had the audacity to say that God told her to do so. I was so confused and hurt, but God told me that he didn't tell her to do it; he allowed her to do it. It was appalling how my friend refused to take the blame, but her betrayal revealed her true colors. Finally, I understood it was time to remove such toxicity from my life.

The enemy comes to steal, kill, and destroy. He will work through anybody or use anything to stop you from your purpose. However, he can't steal what he does not know, so keep your business between you and God. Don't trust everyone until they've shown their loyalty. God allowed my friend to copy my marketing material to remove her from my life and teach me a lesson.

From then on, I learned to keep my plans to myself. Satan uses some people in your life to blatantly manipulate you against God. When you seek God's guidance, he reveals their true face so you can remove them from your life. Satan cannot steal or take anything from you unless God allows it; if he allows it, it is for a bigger purpose. Seeing things from a different perspective can teach you lessons. Instead of blaming God, you humble yourself and accept your mistakes. Otherwise, you're no different from others who refuse to take the blame.

RISE IN PURPOSE

God will bring people into your life for different reasons and seasons. However, he will remove them if they have evil intentions, and those actions will uphold your destiny. Remember, the key to reaching your God-given destiny is in timing, seasons, and obedience. God knows who can go and who can stay until you can discern who is for you and who is against you. Seek Him for guidance through prayer so He can help you.

Chapter 16
God's Glory

"For I know the plans I have for you," declares the LORD, "plans to prosper you and not to harm you, plans to give you hope and a future."

(Jeremiah 29:11)

My journey has led me to a peaceful place where I no longer fear anyone's judgment except God's. People spend their entire lives striving for happiness and peace. No matter how much wealth they build or how successful they get, they always yearn for that inner peace. It can only be achieved through a strong connection with God. After everything I've endured, I don't care who abandons or betrays me.

Once you understand God, you stop questioning his ways. The restlessness is replaced by a sense of ease because you have faith in the best outcome. Once you start following his guidance, you're liberated from the weight of all doubts and uncertainties. You obediently accept what he has in store for you, seek lessons from betrayals, and find a purpose out of your tragedy. *There must be a reason things aren't going my way. God knows best.*

Instead of wallowing in self-pitying thoughts, you start to see the best in every situation. If you fail to accomplish a

RISE IN PURPOSE

goal, you value the experiences based on the lessons you learned. You start to understand that the greater your sufferings, the greater your purpose will be. What's better than being able to serve the purpose God has for you?

When I look back at who I used to be, I only see a wounded soul. I see someone who walked the path with her head down, feeling resentful over things that were out of her control. Instead of looking at the positive aspects of my life, I focused on everything that was wrong. I would have lashed out if someone had told me to find a purpose out of my loss. *Walk a mile in my shoes before you give me your two cents*, I would think to myself.

A person can only take so many hits before they are knocked over. When you've been dragging your feet for years, you can't help but give up. You can't help but laugh at that meaningless advice. No words of comfort are enough to make you see the light at the end of the tunnel. You only fall deeper into the dark pit of despair.

It annoyed me to no end when people, having no inkling of my suffering, advised me to pray and seek God. It was easier said than done. Before I could even consider their suggestion, my mind would put up a barrier of pessimism. How could I connect with someone I couldn't relate with? I tried, but I failed. After multiple failed attempts, I didn't even bother trying. No counseling or support groups could pull me out of the depths of despair. Only God's glory could shine through that impenetrable darkness.

My heart was full of resentment. I harbored an intense hatred for all the pain I experienced. This toxicity only poisoned my own life, hindering my progress and destroying me. Now, I see it was just another step in my journey to bring me closer to God. When we can't find any answers to our desperation, we ultimately seek out God for help. We swallow our pride and start praying in earnest.

I am so humbled and grateful to God for saving me. If I hadn't surrendered to his guidance, I wouldn't have been able to recover. My love for God and my son is interconnected because I found God when I lost my son. I miss Grant with every breath in me, and he will forever live on earth through me. My actions, strength, and compassion will always be a reflection of his soul.

The journey was rough and tough; however, I made it to the other side. Today, I am proud of everything I've overcome. I can hold my head up high. I can proudly claim my success. Instead of succumbing to the darkness in my heart, I fought against my malicious or self-destructive urges. That can't be said for a lot of people, but everyone is on their journey. As long as we're alive, we'll have countless chances to embrace the path of righteousness.

If I can do it, you can too. If I could find it in myself to forgive myself and others, so can you. If I could pull myself together, so can you. If I could resist Satan's temptations, so can you. If I could find my purpose in the great tragedy I encountered, so can you. Despite the horror I experienced,

RISE IN PURPOSE

if I could find faith, so can you. When I managed to detach the roots of grief in my heart, my life was controlled by addictions. If I somehow battled through those urges, I was held back by my fear, hatred, and doubt. When I overcame the vices plaguing my life, a friend would stab me in the back. No matter how hard I tried, my happiness was sabotaged in one way or another. There are too many tragedies in life, so how can we manage to stay optimistic? How can you keep yourself from drowning in the sea of sorrows? That's why we have no other choice than to rely on the power of God.

I know, sometimes, it feels next to impossible to hold on to anything in life, much less something as abstract as faith. When you're not even motivated by the rewards of the world, how can you bring yourself to care about the kingdom of God? It is beyond your understanding. Your grief feeds your despair, and the void keeps growing bigger until the responsibilities of life become too much. Even if you want to try, you fail to fill the suffocating void in your chest. When it all seems so meaningless, turn to God, and he will help you.

During times like this, you need to embrace God. Once you accept you are worthy of his love for you, you can start your journey toward healing. Although we give up on ourselves due to our failures, the same doesn't apply to God. No matter how many times we mess up, we can always turn to God for guidance. As long as we draw breath, we have hope for salvation. Every day is a fresh start, so don't hesitate or wait for an opportunity. Take tiny steps until you feel ready to move mountains. Trust me, you will get there!

Never give up on your dreams, and never rely only on yourself to do anything. When you're lost, it might feel tempting to shun your faith. Even if you keep striving for betterment, you'll eventually find how lost you are without God's guidance. You cannot do anything without God. For those who refuse to believe in the power of God, they might find such statements skeptical. However, such people often complain about the state of restlessness that rules over their minds. Most often, such people fall prey to vices, destructive impulses, and nihilistic thoughts.

When we lose faith in God, life shows us time and again how helpless we truly are. Every time we fall, we get back on our feet, hoping for a different outcome, only to be cruelly put in place by the unfair rules of this universe. All your efforts, optimism, and resilience go in vain. Your grit is meaningless against God's will. Even if you manage to find success somehow, true happiness remains far out of your reach. No matter how hard you try, you just can't seem to find peace of mind. If things are not working out for you, it's a sign.

Lay down your pride, bridge that gap, and pray to God. Initially, you may feel like he can't hear you. You may feel unworthy of his love and attention, but don't give up. Don't

RISE IN PURPOSE

give in to Satan's whispers. If your intentions are pure and if you remain resilient, you'll eventually start to feel God's guidance. Keep praying until he answers. When you struggle against all odds, God acknowledges your strength, and you become one of his bravest soldiers.

I prayed, asking God to bless me with self-confidence, and he did not answer my prayers. Although I felt discouraged, I did not stop asking. Initially, the lack of response filled my heart with despair. I felt beyond exhausted. *Haven't I gone through enough already?* I would think. However, a change in perspective turned things around for me. Despite the negative thoughts, doubts, and desperation, I refused to give up, and he blessed me with something far greater instead—*God Confidence.* He rewarded me for my patience by strengthening my faith. That is how I made it through the wilderness into my promised land.

When you feel desperate, you go around seeking support from anyone but God. Every time you feel lonely, tired, desperate, or hurt, you go around seeking emotional support from people. You forget how we're all flawed beings, struggling through our own problems. You remain skeptical of praying because this doubt overpowers your faith. Your life becomes void of every joy, and despairing thoughts start to plague your mind: *If God loved me, why would he put me through this in the first place?* However, once everyone leaves your side, you soon learn your lesson. You realize you don't need anyone but God to help you, and I am living proof of that. Once you acknowledge this truth, everything starts to fall into place.

All the glory goes to him for helping me become the woman he created me to be. Words are not enough to express my love and gratitude toward him. Despite all the obstacles and challenging circumstances I faced, he gave me the strength to keep going forward. Despite all my fears and doubts, he gave me the courage to navigate through storms. When my burdens got too heavy, he helped me put one foot in front of the other. Every time my faith wavered, he showed me the signs I was looking for. I lost a lot—my family, friends, business, even my religion, but I found God, so the loss is all worth it in the end.

Eternal life is what you should strive for instead of the things of this world. If you're struggling to hold on to faith, you'll find my journey quite relatable in many ways. I know how difficult it is. I don't underestimate anyone's struggle. It takes everything in us to resist that voice trying to lead us astray. It requires determination to remain consistent in your progress, but it is always worth it. This life is only a test of endurance, so we can get to the other side with our hearts purified of all doubts, malice, and fears. If you keep reminding yourself of this eternal truth, it will eventually get ingrained in your brain. Our souls already recognize the light of faith, so you only have to find it again. Search

RISE IN PURPOSE

within your heart, and your righteous actions will start to reflect your beliefs.

When I leave this earth in this body, there is one thing I know for sure: I will see Grant again and finally get to see the voice that led me to Christ and set me free. After everything I've been through, I am beyond grateful that I have the strength to march forward. A part of me can never be recovered. However, I've risen from the ashes, so my faith drives me ahead. I hope this book is an encouragement to you to turn to God, discover your purpose, and become the person He created you to be.

Printed in the USA
CPSIA information can be obtained
at www.ICGtesting.com
LVHW051245151023
761011LV00016B/268